ABOVE THE BATTLEGROUND

The senselessness of conquest is quite apparent from the quiet sphere above the battleground.

A Course in Miracles

ABOVE THE BATTLEGROUND

THE COURAGEOUS PATH TO EMOTIONAL AUTONOMY AND INNER PEACE

STEPHANIE PANAYI

First published by Stephanie Panayi in 2019

Each case study represents a composite of clients and all identifying features have been changed to preserve anonymity.

First edition

ISBN: 9781798514924 (paperback)

Typeset in Crimson by Reedsy

Contents

Introduction

Twenty years ago, I travelled from my home in Australia to the U.S.A. to study a form of bodywork called Rolfing. I'd long had an interest in physical therapy and psychology, and Rolfing seemed to appreciate the mind–body connection. You might expect that going overseas to study would be an exciting prospect for a twenty-four-year-old, but for me it was simply something I knew I *must* do. At that time in my life I experienced significant anxiety, depression, and a sense of grief I couldn't explain. That I was able to get myself together enough to make the journey and complete the training still strikes me as something remarkable. If it wasn't for the strong inner conviction to embark on the venture, I doubt I would have been able to follow through.

Apart from the pull of going overseas to study, I wanted to escape my past and difficult relationships associated with it. It's no coincidence that during my time in the States I came across a book that was all about healing relationships. That book was *A Course in Miracles* — a psycho-spiritual text scribed by Dr Helen Schucman, a research psychologist at Columbia Presbyterian Hospital. Helen began scribing the Course after her colleague at Columbia, Dr William (Bill) Thetford, said emphatically that there must be a way of relating to people that didn't involve the conflict he and Helen experienced between themselves and with other staff members. *A Course in Miracles* was the answer Helen received in her willingness to join with Bill and address his challenge.

I was immediately drawn to the Course when I started reading it. Not long before picking it up, however, I had renounced ever turning to a 'spiritual' book again. I was angry. For many years I had sought solace, inspiration and guidance from books, gurus and workshop facilitators, but nothing and no one had made a lasting impression, or given me something solid to hold on to. I'd concluded that all I had ever read were the opinions of ordinary people as lost in the world as I was. They simply had little problem with claiming authority on a matter.

Nonetheless, I was attracted to the Course, even though I didn't really understand what it was saying. In hindsight, I see my renunciation as the beginning of turning within, a search for my own source of authority and truth, though at the time the only thing I was conscious of was my anger. The Course had an authenticity that was compelling. When reading it I felt connected to something deep within me, and whatever that was, I liked getting in touch with it. I now realise that in the Course I had found something that directed me toward my inner Teacher. In turn, this connection led me to an 'external' teacher who could further facilitate it — I've found the work of the late Dr Kenneth Wapnick to be integral to understanding the Course's message. I am also grateful for Ken's extraordinary personal example.

My study of the Course has run alongside a long-term interest in discovering what makes things tick. As a child, I loved taking watches apart so I could see what was going on beneath the surface. This curiosity regarding the hidden workings of things eventually lead to further study and a degree in psychology and psychophysiology. *A Course in Miracles* has been the unifying influence on my interests, as it has been for this book — it has helped me bring together the insights I've gained from my professional practice and frame them within the context of a 'basic conflict', which (simply stated) relates to our fears of abandonment and punishment, and associated feelings of shame and guilt.[1]

I've found exploring what shame and guilt mean from a psychoanalytic perspective to be extremely helpful: they're not necessarily what the average person assumes them to be. Whether we identify more with shame or with guilt influences every facet of our lives, including our goals, the way we make decisions, and our most pressing emotional needs. It also influences how we relate to our own authority and authority figures generally. Distinguishing between shame and guilt also helps us discern when we are coming from what Eastern philosophies commonly call our 'false' or 'ego' self — that which is identified with incompleteness — as opposed to the wholeness of our spiritual nature.

The purpose of this book is to help us understand how shame and guilt operate in our lives so we can move beyond them and the insecurity they generate. Letting go of shame and guilt enables us to express our innate character and spiritual Self, and this in turn helps us to truly connect with others because we're not relating to them through the distorting lens of neediness. Emotional autonomy leads to an experience of freedom — that our peace isn't contingent on what's happening around us 'on the battleground'.

For those who find solace in the spiritual and aspire to inner peace, it's helpful to see how our habitual thoughts and behaviour prevent us from achieving what we seek through prayer or meditation alone. I also hope this book is accessible to people unfamiliar with *A Course in Miracles*, perhaps with no great interest in metaphysics but with an inclination towards self-inquiry. With this in mind, I've used Jungian concepts to bridge the gap between spirituality and psychology, where a book dedicated solely to discussing *A Course in Miracles* might have expanded upon its metaphysics.

Part of Carl Jung's enduring appeal is his appreciation for both our human and spiritual nature. Jung suggested there are two aspects to our self: one related to our personal history and unique capacities and traits, and another to our transpersonal, spiritual Self that's part of a timeless collective. He proposed that the central task of life is to know ourselves — to get in touch with our 'inner law' and live out our personality, thereby experiencing a sense of wholeness and meaning. He also recognised that this couldn't be achieved without being available to the Self that lies beyond the personality and all its seeming contradictions. One of Jung's major contributions to the fields of psychology and spirituality was to show that embodying our personality and our Self are not exclusive processes — that our sense of wholeness is the outgrowth of a collaboration between the temporal and eternal aspects of our being.

I have also found Jung's concept of a first and second half of life helpful in making sense of the human experience across the lifespan. I've organised this book accordingly, into the morning (Part One: AM) and evening (Part Two: PM) of life, emphasising the challenges in both and the ways in which our emotional dependency and authority problems are played out.

Part One is the purely psychological section, reflecting the emphasis on building a personal identity in life's morning. It looks at how our earliest relationship — that with our parents or primary carers — influences our approach to authority (others' and our own) and our identification with shame and guilt. The work of psychoanalyst Karen Horney is introduced and I apply the idea of shame and guilt *proneness* to her theory of three fundamental 'solutions' to anxiety: the compliant, aggressive, and detached solutions.

Part Two has a spiritual focus and rests largely on the work of Carl Jung. It looks at the major challenges inherent in life's evening, their relationship to our emotional dependency, and introduces the idea of a transcendent Self.

Part Three is the 'how to' section of the book, exploring how to let go of shame and guilt via a process of forgiveness as uniquely defined by *A Course in Miracles*. It concludes with a discussion of the life of one of New Zealand's most celebrated authors, Janet Frame, to illustrate several of the book's major themes.

Facing shame and guilt can be very uncomfortable, however we are often forced to address them through challenging and unexpected circumstances. A period of disorientation in which we feel like we're 'falling apart' is common on the path to emotional autonomy; yet courage to meet our fears will be rewarded with increased happiness and peace as we move from emotional dependency toward an appreciation of our wholeness.

Part One

A.M.

ꕥ

1

Neediness

Whether we want to admit it or not, we are all very needy. We were born that way. Socialisation teaches us how to contain our emotions, to put on a front that says we're unmoved in the face of rejection, ridicule, even praise. Behind the facade, however, we're not far removed from the child who responds to criticism or applause with intense emotion. They just can't put on a poker face. That takes years of training.

Our adult emotional dependency, or 'neediness', stems from our earliest and most profound dependency on the main authority figures in our life — our parents. We depend on our parents for everything, including a sense of security, value and significance. According to how these needs were met, we'll carry some form of emotional dependency into adulthood and into *every* relationship — with people, places, projects and ideologies. The implications are that we can't truly be ourselves while we're invested in fulfilling the unmet emotional needs of the past; nor can we be at peace. Indeed, we'll often find ourselves in conflict with others over meeting these needs.

Am I good enough? Have I done the right thing? These are the core questions related to emotional dependency, and their tendency to loom large in our lives has its origins in a basic conflict.

The Basic Conflict

Psychologists and philosophers have long speculated on the existence of a primary psychological conflict from which all others stem. They've spoken of our need for both freedom and security — of the tension between our desire for self-expression and our dependence on a controlling authority to fulfil some basic needs for our survival.

History is full of events in which this tension is played out — it is the seed of political revolution and sweeping social reform. The philosopher George Hegel, for example, saw the struggle to have our individuality (or 'personhood') recognised as the force leading Europe from serfdom and intellectual bondage under the Church (think, Galileo's imprisonment) to a liberal democracy allowing all people to have a voice.

The freedom to stand apart, follow our aspirations and otherwise express ourselves can, however, turn into narcissistic self-interest if not balanced with concern for the welfare of others. Some form of government regulation is necessary to keep self-interest in check and provide a level of security for all.

Navigating a balance between individual freedom and social control is the challenge of every government. It is also the challenge of every parent in relation to their children. How is the child's need for self-expression balanced with the equally important need to develop self-control? And how, as children, do we manage the inner conflict between our desire to have, do and say what we want and our dependency on our parents for emotional and physical security? When our desires conflict with the wishes of our parents we can feel torn between a need for self-expression and a fear of disapproval and reprisal.

Most of us opt for an unsatisfactory compromise in which our need for security is satisfied at the expense of embodying our whole personality: we shape our behaviour and censor our expression in order to feel safe, and for this we need to feel significant/recognised, and approved of or 'good'. These needs set the basis of our emotional dependency by making us vulnerable to experiencing two of the most distressing 'self-conscious' emotions: shame and guilt.

We rarely spend time contemplating shame and guilt, but we all experience them just the same; they're not exclusive to the criminal, the abuser or the 'bad guy'. History is full of characters we admire for their accomplishments but whose daily lives and relationships reveal another, less appealing side. Aggressiveness, intolerance and self-defeating behaviours are common amongst 'the greats' and show (as the following chapters will illustrate) that they too were subject to the insecurities of shame and guilt.

You mightn't think you experience shame or guilt, or perhaps you're intimately aware of one but not the other. We all experience both. We can feel a sting, for example, if someone greets us without enthusiasm, and an outright attack against us can elicit indignation and anger.

The Inevitability of Conflict

Though the following chapters illustrate how shame and guilt develop within the context of the parent-child relationship, if being able to rid children of shame and guilt was the mark of good parenting, *none of us* would make the grade. It's impossible to create an absolutely anxiety-free environment for a child, and much of this is due to the strikingly different way infants and small children think compared to adults.

French psychologist Jean Piaget pioneered studies showing how a child's perception and understanding is coloured by their limited cognitive development. Of particular relevance to shame and guilt is the finding that, up to seven years of age, a child's thoughts are typically egocentric: children are unable to see a situation from another person's point of view and assume that their thoughts and feelings are the cause of what happens around them. Sigmund Freud called this way of interpreting events 'magical thinking' because it's like believing that uttering a spell will cause someone to die. If a child has hateful feelings or death wishes towards a sibling, for example, they can develop a compulsive need to check on them to make sure they are okay.

Children have difficulty differentiating themselves from what goes on in the world and so take everything personally — if they're not fed on time, it's because of something related to them; if people are angry, happy, sad or absent, that's also because of them. This means that while parenting can certainly help or hinder a child's development, every child begins life geared to take things personally and is vulnerable to experiencing shame and guilt. To a large extent, childhood is a 'set-up' in this regard. To place parenting in its proper perspective, we can aim to be what British paediatric psychiatrist Donald Winnicott called a 'good-enough' parent; one who is committed to their role and understands that children will inevitably face challenges and emotional pain in their lives but can be helped to gain a sense of trust in their ability to manage what comes their way.

Therefore, despite even the most idyllic of upbringings, all of us have identified with shame and guilt to some degree and this will be reflected in patterns of thought, emotions and behaviour. If you find yourself relating to aspects of the following discussion, then you're in good company: perfectly 'together' people, emerging from childhood at peace with themselves and the world, have never existed. The first step in moving toward emotional autonomy — to not needing people to treat us a certain way or for circumstances to be 'just right' in order to feel okay about ourselves — is to look carefully and deeply at our shame and guilt. To experience what we want, we have to first know how we stand in our way.

2

Guilt

Guilt relates to our conscience: if we do something 'bad' (i.e., that breaks an established rule or moral code) we feel guilty and fear punishment. Pioneering children's psychoanalyst Melanie Klein proposed that our earliest experiences of guilt occur in infancy and relate to our complete dependency on our parents: because they can't meet our needs instantly and all the time, we will often feel deprived and angry at them, leading to guilt and a fear of punishment. From the very beginning, our relationship to our parents is ambivalent – we love them when they meet our needs and hate them when they don't.

As we grow older it's not just our anger that makes us feel guilty. We learn all sorts of rules from our parents that, if broken, will result in punishment, and very soon our parents don't have to be around for us to feel guilty – we internalise their messages and establish our own inner parent or 'superego', which embodies the punishing, restrictive messages we have received. Establishing rules is of course necessary for our growth: as children, we need to learn the ropes. Yet unrealistically high parental standards can adversely limit our self-expression and lead to a fear of authority figures in general. To avoid this scenario, some parents use a 'free-range' attitude towards their children, but this can also lead to anxiety since children first need to be contained by others to learn how to contain themselves. Without the ability to 'self-contain' we can fear our lack of control.

Power Plays

Developing emotional and psychological independence from our parents is an essential part of life. It is also one of the most painful and difficult processes we go through because of the tension between needing continuing support from our parents and the desire to develop a sense of our own agency and unique identity. Ideally, we don't want to feel we have to sacrifice one to have the other.

From the toddler asserting a desire to do things their way ('*Me* do it!'), to the teenager beginning to define their own values and preferences, our development requires psychologically differentiating ourselves from our parents. Parents, however, can feel diminished or undermined when this occurs, interpreting their child's move towards independence as a direct attack on their authority. Indeed, classical mythology is full of stories in which parents fear losing power to their children. The Greek god Cronus – son of Uranus (the sky) and Gaia (the earth) – so feared being supplanted by one of his children that he swallowed each of them as they were born.

Mortal parents, likewise feeling threatened but without godly means, can seek to regain their power by becoming overly strict and punitive or by withdrawing attention and affection. This can make us fearful of our initiative and lead to guilt-proneness, particularly if we are also innately sensitive or suffer a traumatic event for which we hold ourselves responsible — for example, if we get hurt while playing in an out-of-bounds area. Fearing their own initiative, a guilt-prone person avoids self-expression. They have decided that the best way to keep people close and stay safe is to be meek and compliant.

The Need to Obey

Obedience to authority is ingrained in childhood, and for some of us the *need* to obey authority figures is very strong and extends well into adult life. This situation was central to Franz Kafka's novel *The Judgement*, which portrays the relationship between a domineering elderly father and his submissive adult son.

Georg Bendemann, is a businessman enjoying success in his work, soon to be married. He visits his father's house and is struck by how large his father still seems, even though Bendemann Senior is now old and frail. Georg carries him to his bed, and all seems well between them, however the emotional atmosphere shifts dramatically when Georg reassures his father that he's tucked in. The old man suddenly becomes enraged, throws back the covers, leaps up onto the bed and accuses Georg: 'You wanted to tuck me in, sunshine, I know that, but I'm not buried yet. And even if it's with my last remaining strength, I'm still enough for you, more than enough for you!'[2] Georg's father continues to berate him, ridicules his business achievements, insults his fiancé and, finally, pronounces: 'And now hear: I sentence you to death by drowning!'[3] Propelled by his father's words and his own guilt into a Pavlovian stimulus-response reaction, Georg runs out of the house and throws himself off a bridge into the river below

Those familiar with Kafka's own relationship with his father will recognise the autobiographical nature of *The Judgement*. Kafka felt harassed and forever diminished by his father, Hermann. A domineering, loud and abrasive character, Hermann was the opposite of his son, who was sensitive and 'bookish'. Kafka took after his mother's side of the family. His father, in contrast, was 'a true Kafka in strength, health, appetite, loudness of voice, eloquence, self-satisfaction, worldly superiority... [and] hot temper'.[4] Kafka often described his relationship with his father as a trial (in the legal sense), and the term 'Kafkaesque' describes a repeating theme in Kafka's body of work: a powerful authority thwarts the protagonist at every turn, perhaps giving him an illusion of justice and freedom, but always totally destroying this illusion in the end.

Kafka knew that part of his father's criticisms of him lay in the fact that Kafka wasn't and couldn't be more like him. In a (hundred-page) letter to his father, Kafka wrote:

> *In any case, we were so different, and in our differences such a danger to each other that, had anyone wanted to predict how I, the slowly developing child, and you, the fully-grown man, would behave towards one another, they could have presumed that you would simply trample me underfoot until nothing of me remained. Well, that did not happen... but maybe something even worse happened...*
>
> *I was an anxious child, and yet I am sure I was also disobedient, as children are, I am sure that Mother spoilt me too, but I cannot believe that I was particularly difficult to handle, I cannot believe that you, by directing a friendly word my way, by quietly taking my hand or by giving me a kind look, could not have got everything you wanted from me.*[5]

Kafka was too afraid of Hermann to say these words directly to him or to hand him the letter himself. He gave it to his mother to pass on instead, although she never did. Georg Bendemann displayed what Kafka felt in relation to his father — a compulsive need to obey and a fear of confrontation. Such is the legacy of life growing up under an authoritarian figure, and a distinct aspect of what psychoanalyst Karen Horney called the 'compliant solution'.

Guilt and the Compliant Solution

For thousands of years people have tried to characterise our differences according to types. In ancient Greece, the physician and philosopher Galen developed a theory of four basic temperaments: sanguine (optimistic and leader-like), choleric (bad-tempered and irritable), melancholic (analytical and quiet) and phlegmatic (relaxed and slow). Many more psychological theories of personality based on the idea that we are born with innate traits have been developed over the years. In the 1950s, for example, Isabel Myers and her mother Kathryn Briggs used Carl Jung's theory on temperaments to devise the Myers-Briggs Type Indicator, a tool that has been used widely to match a person's traits with compatible jobs.

It can be self-affirming to regard some of our characteristics as part of a perfectly normal type because it reinforces that there is nothing right or wrong about our differences. This in itself is valuable, however it can be difficult to determine what is an innate part of our character and what is part of a coping strategy developed over many years in response to our environment. That is, our differences can also be attributed to the dominant psychological defences we use to get by in the world. In terms of what seems to make us 'us', the influence of shame and guilt can be seen in particular behavioural patterns that can be mistaken for innate character types.

Karen Horney, a prominent psychoanalyst in the 1950s, provided insight into three such patterns of behaviour we adopt as children in order to cope with anxiety. She referred to them as the 'compliant', 'aggressive' and 'detached' *solutions*. Horney suggested that we are all primarily motivated by a need to feel secure, and if we experience a lack of love in our early years, we can develop a basic anxiety consisting of feelings of insignificance, inferiority, guilt and an all-pervading sense 'of being lonely and helpless in a hostile world'.[6] Just as the basic *conflict* involves the tension between freedom and security, the basic *anxiety* relates to fear of abandonment and punishment, and can lead us to adopt either the compliant, aggressive or detached solution.

Personal relationships are at the centre of Horney's theory, and the solutions represent a movement either towards, against, or away from others. The compliant person moves *towards* others in an attempt to cling to the most powerful person around them, and they protect themselves from punishment by becoming submissive and 'people-pleasing'. The aggressive person moves *against* others by rebelling and fighting — trying to gain power to minimise feelings of helplessness and inferiority. The detached person moves *away* from others by trying to shut them out of their inner life, withdrawing emotionally. We all express aspects of each solution, however one will be predominant.

The Helper

The guilt-prone person adopts the compliant solution in which they are compelled to please and help others — partly to reassure themselves that they are a *good* person, and also to keep others close. Consequently, they often spread themselves too thin, leading to exhaustion and feelings of being pulled in several directions. In extreme cases they might put aside their better judgement and agree to requests that place them in danger, having dismissed gut feelings for fear of appearing rude, ungrateful or hurting someone's feelings.

Breaking the 'helping habit' isn't easy: intense feelings of guilt and fear of how others mightn't cope without their help are common obstacles. Over-extending ourselves in the service of others can be a way of life; however, we can't tolerate pervasive self-denial indefinitely, and our repressed resentment and frustration will surface in the most inconvenient of ways, often unexpectedly — the panic attack while shopping, or the sudden and inexplicable wave of rage that passes through us while at the office or family gathering. These are signs that something needs an airing and that we need to start tending to our own needs.

This is particularly relevant in the 'helping' professions where Compassion Fatigue is common. The term Compassion Fatigue was coined in the early 1990s to describe nurses' profound physical and emotional exhaustion along with a striking decline in their ability to feel empathy for their patients.[7] A strong risk factor for developing Compassion Fatigue is working with people who have suffered some form of distress similar to our own — it can bring up old wounds that need to be addressed, particularly those surrounding neglect of our needs. Anger, irritability, anxiety, irrational fears, intrusive mental imagery and feeling disconnected from others and our environment are all symptoms of Compassion Fatigue.[8]

Compassion Fatigue affects people from all walks of life. Britain's Prince Harry, for example, has spoken publicly of his mental health issues in a way that illustrates several aspects of Compassion Fatigue. In an interview with Bryony Gordon (2017), the Prince said that his life was 'total chaos' for two years as he battled acute anxiety at royal engagements.[9] Faced with the fight-or-flight response and unable to excuse himself from his surroundings, he was afraid that he might punch someone. Yet Prince Harry couldn't put his finger on the cause of his anxiety.

When he was twenty-eight he began to address his grief over his mother's death. Working with servicemen and women who had suffered immense grief and loss must have brought up the Prince's own buried grief. Anger too emerged because his needs at the time of his mother's death hadn't been appreciated: what had a great impact on him (and was never attended to) was walking behind the gun carriage that carried his mother's coffin in view of thousands of people lining the streets and millions via television. It was something Prince Harry hadn't wanted to do but had felt pressured into.

Anger over not having our own needs met — of not being considered enough in the past — is something that pushes through our best efforts at containment when something in us calls for change. For Prince Harry, working through his grief and anger eventually manifested in a renewed and more dedicated approach to his work and private life.

Power, Success and Happiness: Guilt's Prohibition

> *There are clearly also inhibitions which serve the purpose of self-punishment. This is often the case in inhibitions of occupational activities. The ego is not allowed to carry on those activities, because they would bring success and gain, and these are things which the severe super-ego has forbidden.*[10]
>
> Sigmund Freud

Because our independence and growth in authority can be linked to somehow hurting our parents, each step towards it is met with increasing guilt, even if what we're moving towards is something we really want. This was acutely evident to Freud, who noticed that some people 'occasionally fall ill precisely when a deeply rooted and long-cherished wish has come to fulfilment. It seems then as though they were not able to tolerate their happiness; for there can be no question that there is a causal connection between their success and their falling ill'.[11] Freud described the case of a 'most respectable' academic teacher who for many years had looked forward to succeeding his own teacher and assuming his academic position. When his teacher eventually retired, he found it difficult to accept the role of successor: 'he began to hesitate, depreciated his merits, declared himself unworthy to fill the position designed for him, and fell into a melancholia which unfitted him for all activity for some years'.[12]

Freud suggested that in such cases it is more than simply disillusionment that causes someone to become discontented with their success. Deeper motivations relating to guilt are likely to be operating, and this guilt has its source in the idea that our success or power comes at the cost of 'destroying' or hurting another. Freud experienced this conflict himself while — in his forties — realising his childhood dream of visiting Greece. As he stood on the rocky outcrop at the Acropolis, he felt something odd: instead of being happy at finally fulfilling his childhood wish, he found the whole experience to have an air of unreality and heaviness about it.

Freud decided that he must be perceiving something wrong and forbidden about being at the Acropolis. He concluded that his 'sin' lay in being more successful than his father (a poor and uneducated wool merchant) and in enjoying something that his father wasn't interested in. Standing at the Acropolis, Freud was aware of his autonomy from his father — he had developed his own interests, separate identity and place in the world. The guilt over somehow hurting or diminishing his father by living a life that was authentically his own and in which he had more financial success prevented Freud from enjoying his travel experience.

The idea that our independence is won at the cost of hurting our parents is familiar to children whose parents had a difficult past marked by suffering: they can feel a need to protect them and have trouble detaching as they grow up. Although all their longings might be to move forward and look to the future, they can feel guilty for leaving their parents behind: how, they might reason, can they enjoy themselves and look forward when their parents have had such a hard life, and are perhaps still suffering? The lightness of spirit associated with independence and the discovery of new options and means of expression can therefore prove elusive to people who feel responsible for their parents' happiness.

Playing it Safe

All of us can, at times, be reluctant to take risks. Whether financial, social or psychological, risk-taking is part of any new venture or entrepreneurial process. For some people, an assessment of risk doesn't appear to be as important as the potential for success: instead of seeing the risks associated with starting a venture, they see the opportunities that would be lost if they failed to seize the moment. Most people, however, are risk averse and this is doubly true of the compliant person.

The compliant person's emphasis on avoiding disaster (and therefore their propensity for perceiving it in even the most benign of circumstances) means that even if they manage to get something going, they're prone to meet initial setbacks with fear and blow them out of proportion. Instead of seeing a setback as something to be navigated they decide that it's catastrophic. This is because identification with guilt has them on the lookout for signs of punishment, of everything falling apart. As the compliant person retrieves mail from the letterbox, they dread the bill that breaks the bank, or the tax notice that in effect says 'all that you think you own, you don't, and will now be taken away from you' (a very 'Kafkaesque' scenario!).

The compliant person who is too fearful of self-initiative is likely to seek happiness and fulfilment by creating a romantic ideal of love instead. The lofty notion of 'two becoming one', of losing oneself in a relationship, is held up as a noble cause and a source of hope for personal fulfilment. This romantic ideal of love isn't as lofty as it's made out to be, as what goes by the name of 'love' is very much conditional. Since the compliant person's guilt is never addressed, the amount of reassurance they need to feel loved and lovable will never be enough. They'll be on the lookout for signs of emotional coolness in their partner and become resentful, clingy or despondent if they suspect it.

Defending Against Guilt: Suffering and Self-Sabotage

For the compliant person who *does* manage to move beyond their fear of risk and begin an enterprise, there remains a need to minimise their guilt. Since guilt creates anxiety over future punishment, it is often eased by masochism as a way of atonement. In effect the compliant type self-sabotages, punishing themselves in a seemingly random (or unintentional) way: accidentally scraping the car as they drive into the garage, or cutting themselves while preparing dinner for example.

A common form of self-sabotage is to spend money we know we shouldn't, leaving ourselves short. This scenario was perhaps at the centre of Wolfgang Amadeus Mozart's unending financial troubles: for all his success, Mozart never seemed to have enough money to get by.

Mozart had an intense relationship with his demanding father, Leopold, who ran his career from the time he began performing publicly as a six-year-old, until the age of twenty-five. As a young child, Mozart and his sister Maria Anna ('Nannerl') travelled frequently with their parents across Europe to exploit their prodigious talents. The tours came to an end as both children grew older: the teenage son was too old to be a novelty performer, and Leopold's conservatism dictated that Nannerl stop performing when she was eighteen and 'of marriageable age'.

The first major strain in Mozart's relationship with his father occurred when he was twenty-two years old. Both men had court positions with the Prince Archbishop of Salzburg but were unhappy with several conditions of their employment. They therefore planned a trip out of Salzburg to see if Mozart might find a better position in one of the German courts and make some money performing in Paris. The Archbishop only allowed a leave of absence for Mozart, so his mother, Anna Maria, travelled with him in Leopold's place — for the first time Mozart was travelling without his father.

Though Leopold wasn't among the travelling party, he dictated orders in minute detail via mail, and the letters between father and son give an insight into the dynamics of their relationship. Disappointment and reproach form a major thread through Leopold's letters: try as he might, Mozart didn't find a patron in Germany or gather any significant interest in his work to secure a concert. Upset by Mozart's lack of success, Leopold used self-pity to manipulate him through guilt — Mozart should think of his poor suffering father to whom he owed so much and try harder to ingratiate himself with the powerful upper classes and conform his music to the popular taste.

Leopold's chief complaint was that Mozart's lack of success was due to carelessness, negligence and laziness. This criticism was unfair. Mozart did try to make a go of things, he was simply unlucky and neither the time nor place was receptive to his work. In Paris for instance he wrote a symphony but couldn't get it performed, composed a large part of a ballet but got no credit for it, and wrote a concerto for a duke who left town before paying. The greatest downfall of the trip involved Mozart's mother. Within three weeks of complaining of toothache, a sore throat, and earache, she abruptly passed away.

When the news of his wife's death was relayed to Leopold via a friend at Mozart's request (he wanted to spare Leopold and Nannerl the grief of finding out by mail), Leopold's letters to

Mozart were harsh and unsympathetic. Leopold blamed him for the death of Anna Maria – he insinuated that Mozart wasn't mature enough to have handled the situation properly and that his mother's death was due to his negligence. Mozart's letters to his father are full of pleas for understanding – firstly for the trauma he had gone through in witnessing his mother's demise, and secondly that he had done all he could to fetch a doctor, albeit he arrived too late. Leopold never provided his son with anything resembling absolution. His dominant message was that Mozart wasn't capable of managing anything properly without him.

Another major source of strain in the father-son relationship occurred when Mozart was twenty-five and well and truly fed up with his position as court composer to the Prince Archbishop of Salzburg. The demands of Archbishop Colloredo were stifling. Mozart was directed to produce quaint pieces for Colloredo's evening entertainment, was treated like a servant, and paid poorly. His service ended abruptly after he resigned from his position. True to form, instead of appreciating Mozart's need for greater scope to express his talent (and to be treated with dignity), Leopold berated him for being reckless.

Mozart didn't have the conservative spirit of his father and his need for creative expression was greater. He therefore didn't seek another court position (the enduring form of employment of his father) but moved to Vienna in search of freelance work that would provide more scope for his creativity. In moving to Vienna, Mozart was free of his father's controlling guidance and the debilitating servitude of working under Colloredo. Mozart needed to emancipate himself from such influences in order to let his musical self fully emerge. His father, however, was critical of the move, perceiving him as frivolous and irresponsible for taking on the financial risk of freelance work.

This was to be a theme between father and son — whenever Mozart made an independent move, his father would load guilt upon him. When Mozart announced his engagement to his future wife Constance, Leopold cut him off entirely until after the wedding. Even then, Leopold and Nannerl (always dutifully on the side of her father) refused invitations to meet with the couple: they never embraced Constance or forgave Mozart for going against his father's wishes. This was a great blow to Mozart; letters written by Constance reveal the distress and grief he experienced in response to his father's disapproval.

Mozart's decision to leave Salzburg and try his hand as a freelance composer in Vienna paid off. He became successful, organising a series of subscription concerts that were a sell-out. Ironically, since freeing himself of his father's influence on his career, and able to express himself freely in music, Mozart displayed an entrepreneurial bent that Leopold had always bemoaned was lacking.

Despite Mozart's success, the money never seemed to be enough to make ends meet. The idea that Mozart died in poverty due to a lack of opportunity doesn't hold up to scrutiny. Mozart generally did have money coming in — he earned more than most other musicians at the time — he simply wasn't 'good' with it. He loved new clothes, dressed like an aristocrat, had servants, stabled a horse for riding in the afternoons and lent money to unreliable friends. Though he wasn't a heavy gambler or drinker, no sooner had the money come in than it was gone.

Self-sabotage is a possible explanation for Mozart's money-management issues. The deep association between independence from his father defying him to live according to his own spirit — and guilt meant that he had an unconscious need to sabotage his own happiness. That Mozart remained eternally guilt-ridden is evident in letters he wrote in the last year of his life.[13] He also suffered from frequent periods of profound sadness and emptiness, which might also explain his 'Champagne tastes on a beer budget': a compulsion to surround himself with beautiful, refined things he couldn't afford was perhaps a measure of his need to defend himself against a sense of inner poverty and depression (which is extraordinary considering the richness of his compositions — an irony explored later in Chapter Six).

Leopold undoubtedly loved his son but was likely plagued with feelings of emptiness himself when he lost what he thought had given him purpose and significance in his life — his role as manager of his son's career. Ultimately, Leopold couldn't stand the thought of his son's autonomy. His endless recriminations were a way of both undermining Mozart's autonomy ('you can't do anything properly without me') and punishing him for it. Unable to accept any role in his own unhappiness, Leopold placed the cause squarely on the shoulders of his 'ungrateful, frivolous, irresponsible' son.

Perfectionism is another way the compliant type can hurt themselves. Self-berating and doubting are ways they undermine themselves, sapping their energy without them being aware of the cause: *Why is it that I can be full of enthusiasm in one moment, depressed and disinterested the next?* Guilt for their achievement is what makes them counter a forward creative move with a self-destructive one. Horney gives the example of a writer, at first happy with their work but then caught in a spiral of self-defeating thoughts and fault-finding which leaves them unable to work for several days.[14]

They can further sabotage their endeavours by falling back into old patterns of helping others at the expense of their own enterprise. The guilt-prone or compliant person has to fight against their need to keep themselves down, which often manifests in minimising the quality and importance of their work. This attitude prevents them from tapping into their resources because they are ambivalent about their potential success. Indeed, they can feel an oppressive futility in what they do that has no relation to reality itself or the true opportunities available to them. The guilt-prone person has the challenge of moving through the inertia and working towards lifting themselves up.

The compliant person is in a real bind when it comes to their success: they become disturbed when things are difficult because they fear impending doom, but they also get anxious soon after things go well. This is because of the role suffering plays in keeping guilt-anxiety away. It's also the reason that Horney gives for the compliant solution being the least satisfactory: all three solutions involve suffering, but the compliant person feels miserable more often and more intensely than others because suffering is at the core of the very solution itself.

3

Shame

While guilt-anxiety relates to a fear of punishment for crossing a line, shame-anxiety relates to our need to feel valued. Shame, like guilt, involves self-condemnation, however it's not about feeling good or bad, but feeling weaker, smaller, inferior. Shame is about not being *good enough* and is based on feelings of exclusion and of falling short of an ideal. In other words, shame comes from comparing ourselves to others. It's the inner voice that tells us the reason we find something difficult is that we're just not smart or talented enough. It's the voice that tells us we don't belong.

Shame is based on the type of anxiety we feel as infants when our parents withdraw from us emotionally or physically, and relates to a fear of abandonment. Our extreme dependency on our parents means that any sense of deprivation is frightening. If we don't get fed when we're hungry, and our screams don't get us what we want, then we feel we're on precarious ground. Not only are we met with the reality of our helplessness, but we feel inadequate to attract the care of others and experience a sense of abandonment which is deeply painful.

If our pain is significant and frequent enough, we can become ashamed of our emotional vulnerability and begin a 'toughening up' process that begets a lack of empathy in later life. Psychologist John Bowlby's attachment theory also describes how feelings of abandonment in childhood can lead to fear of new environments and situations in later life, or overt hostility or cool detachment towards our partners if we've felt abandoned by them — reacting to them as we're likely to have reacted to our parents. To protect us from being overlooked and discarded we can become preoccupied with achieving status, power and recognition.

The Chosen One

A sense of abandonment doesn't have to relate to physical separation. Children can feel discarded if a parent ignores them or seems preoccupied. Such feelings can emerge alongside a growing awareness that our parents share an intimacy that we're not a part of — that they are part of a world of adults, with adult concerns and responsibilities from which we are excluded. This sense of exclusion is particularly stark for children of Holocaust survivors who grow up under the pervasive backdrop of their parents' shared history, one which the children aren't a part of and (in the child's mind) can never make up for. With their own existence not being enough to draw their parents out of their darkness, children can decide that they themselves aren't *enough*: they're not the preoccupation of their parents' lives, their parents' (exclusive) past is.

The need to possess the exclusive love and attention of both or one of our parents is something that we all deal with as children and is reflected in our adult relationships. Sibling rivalry can also play a major role in our sense of abandonment — if parents seem to favour other siblings, we can begin to question our value. As Freud noted, the family home provides a fertile ground for feeling passed over in favour of someone or something else:

> *There are only too many occasions on which a child is slighted, or at least* feels *he has been slighted, on which he feels he is not receiving the whole of his parents' love, and, most of all, on which he regrets having to share it with brothers and sisters.*[15]

And even if there are no siblings to compete for the affection of our parents, we are always competing with the attention they give each other, whether such attention reflects an all-consuming love, or an equally consuming hate.

We all have a fantasy of being the chosen one. I'm reminded of the sporting adage: 'Second is the first loser'. Instead of fearing anger and punishment as the guilt-prone person does, the shame-prone person fears contempt and rejection. But just as the guilt-prone person sees themselves according to the dichotomy of all good or all bad, the shame-prone person also sees themselves along binary lines — if they're not number one, then they're nothing at all.

The need for attention isn't simply narcissistic. Attention is vital to consolidating our sense of self in our first five years of life, a process fundamental for healthy psychological and emotional growth. This was highlighted by the plight of children in Romanian orphanages during the Soviet era. After the fall of the Soviet regime in 1989, the conditions of the orphanages were exposed: babies and children received perfunctory care in the form of food and shelter, but no thought was given to their emotional and psychological needs — they were not being held or sung to, for example. Spending their time in cribs and with little stimulation from the outside world, these orphans were unable to develop a sense of self (let alone a *positive* sense of self) from their environment. Intellectual deficits and emotional problems into adulthood were severe.[16]

Our sense of self develops as we see ourselves reflected in others' responses to us and in our affects upon the environment, during play and creative activities for example. Often a child's need for recognition ('look at me!') is so great that they will behave badly in order to attract a parent's attention, even if that attention comes in the form of punishment. The fear of abandonment is like a fear of emotional starvation.

Our need to be seen permeates our day-to-day world. In *How to Win Friends and Influence People* — a best-selling business guide of 1936 — Dale Carnegie paints a picture of people as creatures thirsting for approval and prone to defensiveness in the face of criticism. The main point of Carnegie's book is that when trying to win someone over, it is vital to remember that they are first and foremost a creature of emotion rather than logic. The deepest urge in human nature, says Carnegie, is a rarely satisfied longing for significance. Therefore, the key to getting someone to do what you want is to make them feel *important*. In other words, if you protect someone from feelings of insignificance, you've made an ally. Unsurprisingly many have found Carnegie's techniques to work like magic.

Shame and the Aggressive Solution

If a child feels unloved, second best or humiliated they can decide to block off loving feelings to protect themselves. This is the case in Horney's aggressive solution which involves 'moving against' others, and is characteristic of shame-prone people. Pushing someone away is an act against dependency. It's a way of saying, 'I don't love you; I don't *need* you'. But of course, the last thing a child wants is for their parent to actually abandon them. There is often a frustrating contradiction in people ashamed of their dependency: they push people away then plead for them to come back.

While the compliant person fears their own ambition and success, the aggressive person dreads helplessness and despises dependency. To avoid it, they will do all they can to become powerful or to otherwise feel bullet-proof, and project their disdain for their own emotional vulnerability onto others who they perceive as being overly sensitive. They might also exploit people, rationalising it as self-defence: it's a dog-eat-dog world and so you must exploit or be exploited.

Moreover, while the compliant, guilt-prone person fears expressing their authority, idealising the concept of love instead, the aggressive person fears intimacy and so despises softness (yet paradoxically can be drawn to it in a partner). They search for satisfaction in recognition, power and mastery. They idolise the concept of willpower and don't have a problem with exerting their influence in the world or in being *the* authority; their solution demands it of them. In fact, the aggressive person *despises* authority figures and doesn't like being told what to do, reacting with hostility and frustration in environments where there is a controlling dynamic, such as at school, in the workplace, or even waiting at a set of traffic lights. Cut them off on the freeway at your peril — they'll see this as a sign of disrespect, an attack on their importance. They can also be extremely contrary — you say 'black', they will invariably say 'white'.

The aggressive person is unsettled by intimacy because they

fear being truly seen. Since close relationships require some intimacy to be sustainable, the aggressive type can experience them as a significant source of frustration — they might want someone in their life yet find it difficult to be vulnerable and honest enough to achieve real closeness. Indeed, they commonly feel claustrophobic in a relationship as it grows in intimacy, at which point they might assert their need for freedom — to go where and with whom they please. Addiction to pornography can also stem from these needs: objectifying people as sex objects can be a form of distance management.

Feeling rejected or humiliated, this type is prone to react with 'narcissistic fury'.[17] This is different to the righteous indignation of a compliant person when they feel unfairly accused of something ('I did not!'). The aggressive person's anger can appear inexplicable, wild, explosive. The powerful role that shame plays in acts of aggression without a seeming cause was highlighted in a paper by Dr Joseph Satten, a veteran in the field of forensic psychiatry. In 'Murder without Apparent Motive' Satten examined men convicted of seemingly unmotivated murders. The men had become 'triggered' when they felt rejected by the victim. For example, one of the men, a labourer, had strangled a teenager when he rejected his sexual advances. Another, an army corporal, beat to death a young boy because he imagined the boy was making fun of him.

The men themselves couldn't understand why they killed these strangers, but all had suffered significant deprivation and cruelty when young and were terrified about being considered 'sissy' or physically small. Their unconscious rage was ignited when the victim-to-be unwittingly triggered the sense of humiliation first experienced at the hands of people more powerful than them. As Adrian Bailey, a man recently convicted of numerous brutal sexual assaults in Australia, had said to a victim, 'look who's got the power now'.[18] Bailey had also been abused as a child, and during a police interview over the murder of his last victim — Jill Meagher —expressed shame for crying, calling himself 'a big sissy man'. In his testimony, he said that as he was passing Jill (who was unknown to him) in the street he started talking to her because he thought she looked 'lost' and 'distraught'. Jill indicated she was fine and kept walking, however Bailey felt she was 'flipping him off' and became enraged.

We *all* operate under the influence of shame to varying degrees. If we've ever been rejected for a job, passed over for promotion or refused entry into a nightclub, we might recall a sense of indignation and an impulse to retaliate. But if we have enough of what psychologists call 'ego-strength' — a relatively secure and positive sense of self — we can withstand outer assaults to our pride without feeling overwhelmed by retaliatory feelings. Sometimes we manage, sometimes we don't. But when we don't, our capacity to rein ourselves back in is also a function of ego-strength. For the people in Satten's study, there was no turning back once the horse had bolted.

Not all aggressive types are criminals, but they are all narcissistic, sharing a need for recognition and to exploit others. While these characteristics are true of aggressive types generally, Horney points to three sub-types that explain some defining differences: the narcissistic type, the perfectionistic type and the vindictive type. These subtypes explain why not all aggressive types appear buoyantly positive, or misanthropic, or bent on revenge.

The Buoyant Narcissist

We all know people who display a 'can do' attitude no matter the task. Their positivity and achievements can be a source of inspiration. For some of these 'achievers', however, their boundless self-belief stems from an overestimation of their abilities based on a need to feel powerful and in control. Horney's narcissistic type isn't afraid to wear their high self-regard on their sleeve. They adore their grandiose self-concept and this attitude seems to give them unlimited self-confidence.

It's very rare for narcissistic types to express any self-doubt and in contrast to the compliant person they seem to have an infinite capacity to overlook their flaws and shortcomings, often reasoning them into virtues. It's not that they're unscrupulous in business for example, but they are *savvy*. When the shoe is on the other foot, however, they become indignant with rage. Breaking promises, defrauding and being unfaithful are common scenarios involving this double-standard.

The narcissistic type can be charming and gives the impression of loving people in general: they are happy to do favours, readily flatter people and can be generous. In return they need admiration and devotion to confirm their self-belief, and this leads to difficulties in close relationships: spouses and children are often critical of them for their lack of consideration and warmth at home. It's not uncommon therefore for the narcissistic type to feel more comfortable with friends and outsiders who 'understand' them. As epitomised by Shakespeare's King Lear, their need for ostentatious displays of love (more than love itself) makes them susceptible to the manipulations and schemes of sycophants, often leading to their downfall.

Like aggressive types as a whole, the narcissistic type doesn't function well in environments structured by other people — whether that be as a student in a classroom, an employee, working to another person's schedule, or as a guest (and not the host) of a party. In many cases they like to hold the floor in a conversation, often cutting across others to keep themselves and their agenda in the foreground, boasting whenever they see an opportunity. Unlike the compliant person who *underrates* the importance of their activities or projects, the narcissistic type *overrates* the importance of theirs and is unashamedly a self-promoter.

As is also true of aggressive types generally, the narcissistic type is a boundary violator. The right of another to their own values, beliefs, preferences, thoughts, emotions and personal space are all things that go unconsidered by narcissist types. While the compliant person's relatively weak boundaries lead them to become quickly and deeply enmeshed with the emotions and problems of others, the aggressive person tends to ride roughshod over others' feelings, thoughts and personal space — making inappropriate comments about an employee's appearance, for example, or ignoring their need for privacy or right to do things their own way. Like an authoritarian parent, they have difficulty seeing their 'subordinates' as individuals with their own temperament, character and aspirations.

The aggressive type's need for independence and expression of initiative means that many are found amongst the ranks of entrepreneurs — people who see an opportunity for innovation in business and begin a new enterprise. Personal satisfaction and the need for independence are two main motivators for beginning an entrepreneurial venture, but things turn sour when a significant underlying purpose is to make up for feelings of insignificance. Psychoanalyst and entrepreneurship scholar

Manfred Kets de Vries described these entrepreneurs as having a 'reactive narcissistic disposition' and they have many characteristics consistent with Horney's narcissistic type. Kets de Vries calls them 'reactive' because though they present a convincing facade of supreme self-confidence, they respond either with rage or bouts of depression when things don't go as they like . As Horney noted of her narcissistic type, their resilience gives them 'a capacity to bounce', *up to a point:* repeated failures or rejections can cause them to self-destruct as their underlying feelings of unworthiness surface.[19]

Kets de Vries concluded that many entrepreneurs have feelings of insecurity and inferiority that they try to counteract with excessive control and activity.[20] Though their surface grandiose self-concept makes them appear buoyantly optimistic, the narcissistic type isn't immune to emotional ups and downs: their behaviour can have a bi-polar quality in which a manic phase of action is followed by one of mild depression. When they are 'up' they are really up, intoxicated with the idea of achieving higher status and power to an extent that can lead to excessive risk-taking. Kets de Vries refers to this manic phase as a 'flight into action' or 'manic defence'. It's not unlike the manic defence of consumerism which many of us employ from time to time — we get hooked on the idea of purchasing a certain product and our external focus helps us avoid an uncomfortable inner reality.

When things go *very* badly in their business or personal life, the veneer of extreme self-confidence can crumble and mild depression is replaced with utter hopelessness. Friends and associates are often taken aback that the person they knew to be so positive and full of life could reach such depths of despair. And since the narcissistic type views feelings of depression, anxiety, hurt or hopelessness as signs of weakness, they often keep them to themselves and this contributes to feelings of isolation. Self-destructive behaviour such as alcohol abuse is a common result.

Kets de Vries gives the example of a client, 'Mr. X', who fits the profile of a reactive entrepreneur. Mr. X was a forty-four-year-old father of four children, who sought counselling after separating from his wife of twenty-one years. He had been used to denying any depressive feelings through unrealistic optimism, humour, excessive activity and control, and by turning to self-help books or business journals with a positive motivational emphasis. At the time he sought counselling, however, the bubble of contrived optimism had burst: Mr. X's business wasn't doing well, he didn't like living on his own, and was depressed. He felt completely worthless and that life had no prospects. At work he was consumed with negative thoughts about how his creditors and customers would gloat about his failure, and he worried about how is mother and other family members would react.[21]

Mr. X was the youngest of six children. His father had been an emotionally distant figure who died when he was eight, and he described his mother as cold and critical — nothing he did was ever good enough; he had never been able to live up to her standards. As the youngest he felt neglected, easily dismissed, and was tormented and criticised by his older siblings. Mr. X's workaholic behaviour, his need to keep busy, and his desire to control all aspects of his business was driven by a great need for admiration and approval from his parents.[22]

The high self-regard Mr. X wore on his sleeve was a cover for the ever-present threat of depression from not feeling good enough. Unaware of how these childhood conflicts were playing out in his life, he treated his employees in much the same way he had felt treated by his parents and siblings. While Mr. X had a master plan for his business, the basis for many of his decisions came from his 'inner theatre'. His irrational behaviour permeated all aspects of the company, influencing its culture, strategies, decision making, goals and values. It was also setting the company up for failure.

Through counselling, Mr. X became aware of what he was acting out at work and in his relationship with his wife. He realised that in order to feel secure he didn't need to control his wife, and that her need for independence and growing assertiveness didn't mean that she was controlling him, nor did it mean she didn't love him or couldn't also be affectionate. He also made a strong effort to empathise with his mother; to understand what it might have been like to suddenly be a widow with six children. Through developing empathy, he was able to take her past behaviour less personally and their relationship improved, giving him more peace of mind. He also became less controlling at work, making sure he gave employees space to work independently, and was better able to tolerate someone disagreeing with him.

Another major change through therapy, was Mr. X's ability to rein in potential 'flights into action'. As he realised that his constant need to speed up the company's growth was driven by a need for power and prestige and was related to key themes in his past, he became more balanced in his actions.[23] By being mindful of his tendency towards compulsive striving and the reasons for it, Mr. X was able to 'slow down and pan out'. This not only made for more rational strategy-making, but gave him the space to become more interested in the development of his employees, eventually taking on a mentoring role.

The Intolerant Perfectionist

Compliant types are often perfectionists because of their need to please and their fear of judgement: whatever they are asked to do, they must do to the highest standard because they interpret their mistakes in catastrophic terms. Aggressive types can also be perfectionists, but the driving force behind their perfectionism is pride for their high standards: they relish being *better, greater* than others. In contrast to the narcissistic type, they want respect rather than glowing admiration (which they tend to scorn). They also (often cruelly and unreasonably) extend their demand for perfection towards others.

The composer Ludwig van Beethoven displayed many characteristics of this type. He held himself to very high standards in his art, worked diligently, was totally sure of his talent and had a sense of mission: to feed the spirit of humanity through his music. He was, however, utterly unmoveable regarding the form in which humanity must accept it. While Mozart wrote music for all manner of people — the musically educated and uneducated — and paid very close attention to the demands and limitation of his singers and instrumentalists, Beethoven composed without these considerations. Beethoven wasn't interested in what other people could appreciate; they must push themselves to accommodate the greatness of his creations.

Beethoven's life-long pattern was to insist that people meet his expectations. When conducting, he would hurl abuse at musicians who had difficulty with his work, and in one case an entire orchestra — tired of his incessant bullying — refused to play for him. His private pupils suffered no less: if a piano student made a mistake, they'd receive a hard pinch or be whipped across their hands with a steel knitting needle.

Beethoven's demands for perfection from others spilled into every aspect of life. When served the wrong meal at a Viennese tavern, he tipped it over the waiter's head. Basically, Beethoven couldn't imagine what it might be like to walk in someone else's shoes.

Adding to his difficulties in 'public relations', Beethoven had a profound lack of self-awareness. In his later years, for example, his appearance became increasingly dishevelled and he kept his composer's room in total disarray; yet when friends would visit, finding him standing amongst the filth and chaos, he would go on about how orderly he was. And though Beethoven was dishonest in business, he saw himself as beyond reproach. Instead, he was paranoid that people, including his friends, were cheating him (and that his stomach trouble was caused by his maid poisoning him). Most remarkably, for all his harshness toward people, Beethoven maintained that he could never bring himself to offend anyone.

Beethoven also didn't take kindly to criticism. Because the aggressive perfectionist believes they are fair, infallible and more virtuous than others, they can't stand to think they might be wrong. Indeed, Beethoven was known to totally and irreconcilably cut ties with very close friends if they disagreed on a subject important to him, his esteem turning to disapproval. For Beethoven, there was a distinct split between love and hate, virtue and vice — he couldn't tolerate contrary feelings towards others, and so saw them in black and white terms; as all good or all bad. In the romantic arena, this type can switch abruptly from being violently in love with someone to being incapable of feeling anything towards them at all: that person is 'dead to them', as Beethoven's father Johann became to him when Beethoven left home.

Beethoven was unmoved when he heard of his father's death and didn't attend his funeral. Unlike Mozart who worked to maintain the remaining fragments of his relationship with his father, Beethoven closed himself off to his. This was likely the result of the controlling brutality of Johann, who had punished Beethoven with beatings and by locking him in the basement when he was a child. From the time he was six, Beethoven was forced to practice the clavier daily and for long hours. According to Alexander Thayer's *The Life of Beethoven*, neighbours remembered Beethoven as 'a tiny boy, standing on a little footstool in front of the clavier... weeping'.[24] Johann sought to profit from his son's talent, and returning home drunk at night would often pull Beethoven out of bed and force him to practice.

Music had been literally beaten into Beethoven by Johann, whereas Mozart had — despite his father's manipulations and incessant criticisms of him as a young man — a relatively close relationship with his father in his formative years. Beethoven's harsh, uncompromising and insensitive approach to others was a case of history repeating itself: he replicated his father's behaviour in many ways.

As is often the case when one parent is despised, Beethoven idealised his other parent — his kindly mother. She was, in his mind, all good; his father, all bad. His perception of women generally was also skewed into two distinct camps: those of 'high virtue' whom he worshipped, and those of low virtue whom he disdained. This 'virgin or vamp' view of women was to lead to years of torment for his nephew Karl and for Karl's mother Joanna. Beethoven had vehemently disapproved of his brother's marriage because Joanna had been five months pregnant at the time of their engagement. Some years after the marriage,

Joanna then committed what Beethoven regarded as the most unpardonable of sins — adultery. Beethoven refused to speak to anyone accused of having committed adultery, and with this offence in Joanna's history, he felt entitled after his brother's death to seek sole custody of his ten-year-old nephew.

Beethoven's status as a renowned composer ensured his success at court. He obtained full custody of Karl and was a heavy guardian. He had friends spy on Karl's movements away from home, harassed Karl about his friends (they weren't good enough), his ambitions to be a soldier (again, not good enough), and in his twentieth year Karl broke under the pressure. He bought two pistols and attempted suicide but survived. When asked why he had wanted to die, he replied: 'Weariness of imprisonment'.[25] Later, Karl told a magistrate that Beethoven 'tormented him too much', always pushing him to 'be better'.[26] Beethoven's main concern at the time — at least the main concern he expressed — was for himself. He had a propensity to feel hard-done-by at the hands of others (often referring to himself as 'poor Beethoven'), and on this occasion he expressed distress and anger for the 'disgrace' Karl's suicide attempt had brought to him.

The Entitled Vindictive Type

The vindictive type doesn't just have a need to win; they have a need to get even. While all the aggressive types enjoy vindictive triumph, the vindictive type experiences an overwhelming and intense desire for it: vindictiveness energises them and is a significant motivator in directing the course of their life. As Horney puts it, this type lives 'for the day of reckoning'.[27] Rather than seeing their vindictiveness as a negative, they are convinced it is a strength, often bragging about their vindictive exploits to others.

This type is the 'coolest' of the aggressive types in terms of emotional warmth, and where the need for vengeance can be checked somewhat by love or self-preservation in the narcissist and perfectionist, the vindictive type's impulse towards revenge outweighs anything else. Monomania is the result: a fanatical and blinkered pursuit of their goal with no sense of proportion. Horney suggests Captain Ahab, in Herman Melville's *Moby Dick*, is a prime example of monomania in action. The captain becomes focussed on revenge after his leg is torn off by a great white whale during a whaling voyage. Ahab disregards the love of his wife and child to set sail again to fulfil his mission, and when the whale is finally sighted he is so overwhelmed with hatred that he becomes reckless, gets tangled in the line of his harpoon and is dragged to the bottom of the ocean by his nemesis.

Aside from revenge, a strong need to triumph over others makes this type extremely competitive. They can't stand it if anyone knows more or achieves more than they do and will compulsively try to drag them down. Achieving this aim is their priority and they can be treacherous in its pursuit; however, they pride themselves on their honesty and fairness even though they don't embody either of these qualities. They reason that if something serves their self-interest then it is true, fair and honest because *they* are a good person, more honest and fairer than others. The vindictive type convinces themselves that the end (the preservation of a worthwhile person like themselves) justifies the means.

A sense of entitlement is another marked characteristic of the vindictive type. They feel entitled to having their needs met and to disregard those of others, to criticising but not being criticised, and to being an exception to rules that other people follow. If they *are* held accountable, they are likely to feel unfairly treated and seek revenge.

All of these traits — the tendency towards monomania and revenge, extreme competitiveness, a sense of entitlement and an inability to acknowledge personal flaws — have been exhibited by the forty-fifth president of the United States, Donald Trump. In his book, *Think Big,* Trump devotes a whole chapter to revenge and how much he loves 'getting even' with people, advocating 'screwing them back' many times over.[28] The extent to which revenge is part of Trump's 'raison d'être' is highlighted in a passage from the British entrepreneur Richard Branson's autobiography *Finding my Virginity*. Invited, unexpectedly, to lunch at Trump's apartment, Branson was taken aback by the subject of Trump's relentless focus during their meeting: he wanted to talk about five people he planned to take revenge on for not helping him financially when he needed it.[29]

True to the vindictive type, though Trump can't tolerate people treating him in a way he thinks is unfair, he reasons that it's okay for him to use fraud and deception to cheat others. Not only has he been known to swindle investors and others in the business realm, but he has a track record for not paying workers and refusing to pay for goods and services already delivered.[30]

The source of this sense of entitlement, according to Horney, is feeling belittled at the hand of parents or other primary caregivers during childhood — the vindictive type didn't get the positive attention they needed to feel special, so now they demand it of the world in an attempt to fulfil the unmet needs of the past: 'I'm a special case, an exception to the rules'. Their childhood is likely to have been extremely difficult and may have involved physical abuse, humiliation, derision and neglect. While not a lot is known about the details of Donald Trump's upbringing, it's clear that his workaholic father (also a 'shady' business man, as was his father before him) was a formidable, stern and critical patriarch who pushed his sons relentlessly toward success in the family business. Trump's mother was a more distant figure than his father, enjoying managing her opulent home, volunteering and luncheons.

Whatever the cause of Trump's vindictive nature, troubling behaviour was evident in his early years. There are neighbours' accounts of Trump throwing rocks at little children in playpens and provoking fights, and his behaviour was so unruly as a teenager that his father sent him to a military academy to develop discipline.[31]

In his book *The Making of Donald Trump*, investigative journalist David Cay Johnston describes a situation suggesting Trump inhabits the cooler end of the emotional warmth spectrum. Two days after Trump Senior died, aged ninety-three, Donald Trump's nephew, Fred, and his wife had a baby boy, William. Soon after birth, William began having frequent seizures and other health complications. He needed significant continuing medical intervention and the associated bills ran into hundreds of thousands of dollars. Fred and his wife Linda didn't have the vast financial means enjoyed by the rest of the Trump clan, and so they relied on the medical insurance plan that had been established by Trump Senior — through his company — for the whole family. A letter from the family lawyer had instructed the medical plan to cover all of William's costs.

Trouble began when Fred and other grandchildren discovered that they'd only been left a token amount of money in Trump Senior's will. They filed a lawsuit claiming their grandfather had been unduly influenced by Donald and his siblings. Donald struck back by ceasing all medical benefits for William. When pressed to consider the cruel nature of his actions, Donald refused to acknowledge any wrongdoing or cold-heartedness.

According to Horney, much of the vindictive type's coldness towards others stems from a defensive emotional hardening to protect their sense of vulnerability and weakness, which is reminiscent of the discussion in Chapter Two on shame and crimes without apparent motive. The need to say — metaphorically or otherwise — 'Look who's got the power now' — is central to vindictiveness. Indeed, Horney suggests that all sadistic trends have vindictive needs behind them.[32]

In conclusion, all three aggressive solutions are narcissistic in their disregard for others, and all aim for a sense of mastery in life. The quest for mastery gives them a certain zest for living, however the ways in which each of these solutions tries to achieve this sense of mastery is different: the narcissistic type works to impress and charm; the perfectionistic type demands perfection of themselves and others; and the vindictive type strives for revenge. Horney also distinguishes between the aggressive types in terms of their capacity for emotional warmth towards others: the narcissistic type is the warmest of the three; the vindictive type the chilliest.

There is of course hope for those who embody any of the above characteristics, which all of us do to a certain degree. Just as the guilt-prone person can move beyond their fear of catastrophe and enjoy the energy and sense of purpose that comes from playing an authoritative role, the shame-prone person can move beyond their fear of intimacy and emotional vulnerability, welcoming the warmth and sense of communion that comes from deeply caring for others.

Shame and Self-Destructive Behaviour

Horney's aggressive types all reach for self-aggrandisement and on the whole exhibit a desire for self-preservation and triumph. Others whose identity is significantly linked with shame display a 'bring it on' attitude toward physical danger and their own demise.

The life of Patty Schemel, outlined in her memoir *Hit So Hard* is a good example of this. Schemel was the drummer for Courtney Love's rock band Hole, which achieved commercial and critical success in the 1990s. Her story is also useful in showing that not all shame-prone people are attention-seekers, self-promoters or 'go-getters' in the usual sense: they don't have a conscious glorified, narcissistic self-concept in defence of an unconscious shameful one. On the contrary, they're all too aware of their feelings of unworthiness and seek out drugs, amongst other things, to obliterate those feelings.

Schemel was the middle child of three and grew up in a small town in the United States. Her childhood was unconventional in that her parents would often host Alcoholics Anonymous meetings in their living room — Schemel and her siblings listening in on the stories of addiction and recovery. Both of Schemel's parents never relapsed, however a genetic vulnerability for substance addiction may have been passed on to her — something that became manifest when adolescence loomed and she entered fifth grade at school. Schemel had red hair and wore glasses — common targets for mockery growing up in the Seventies. Boys overtly laughed at the thought of 'going with' her and Schemel had the added difficulty of a growing awareness that her sexuality strayed from the norm: she got the message from the wider culture that she should be ashamed of herself.[33]

Schemel began to feel stupid in public. She felt lonely and suffered social anxiety. She also had a reputation for being stubborn and a propensity for angry outbursts. By the time she was twelve, she had learnt to self-medicate with alcohol on a regular basis. She first got drunk when she was eleven and enjoyed the relief of not feeling awkward or angry; she felt calm, fearless and attractive; she finally felt 'at home'.[34]

Around the same time Schemel started drinking, she began playing the drums — the aggressiveness of drumming appealed to her, as did the 'violence' of punk music; she had a lot of unchannelled anger. Schemel also counteracted her feelings of vulnerability and awkwardness by making people laugh: they would enjoy spending time with her and she could feel okay about herself for a while. When she landed the role of drummer for Hole when she was twenty-five, she also stepped into the role of group-comedian. She was well-liked, but while she managed to stop drinking for several months leading up to the recording of *Celebrity Skin* in 1998, her time in the recording studio was to be traumatic.

Celebrity Skin was produced by Michael Beinhorn who, unknown to Schemel, had a reputation for taking the recording band's drummer off recordings and replacing them with his own session player. Beinhorn had no intention of allowing Schemel to play the drums on the final recording, but rather than tell her of his plans, he tried to break her so that she would resign. As Schemel played the drum parts that she herself had written, Beinhorn would say they weren't good enough and make her play them again, and again, for eight hours straight, one day to the next. (One of the technicians later told Schemel that Beinhorn turned the sound off and read the paper while she played.)

Schemel couldn't understand what was wrong with her playing.

Adding to her confusion and frustration was the fact that none of her bandmates came to her defence. Schemel refused to give in. Exhausted, she kept on playing until Beinhorn 'broke' and finally told Courtney Love to take Schemel off the recording. Schemel was gutted. She had been sober for months, but after leaving the studio — feeling humiliated, betrayed, confused and her artistry questioned — she reached for comfort in drugs. She left the band and rented a room where no one (including her family) could find her.

Schemel's drug and alcohol use went to a level it hadn't gone to before: she became addicted to heroin and crack. She became homeless, turning to theft, prostitution and selling drugs to feed her habit. Not only was the addiction a means of numbing her emotional pain, Schemel's self-destructive behaviour was a (self-confessed) 'Screw you, guys!' towards everyone who had let her down. In her demise she pointed an accusing finger at all who had abandoned and mistreated her in her near present and distant past. There was, therefore, a strong element of self-pity in her self-destructiveness, along with a tacit agreement of the lowly opinion she believed others had of her.

Not many who reach the depths of Schemel's addiction survive to tell the tale. Fortunately, Schemel experienced a moment of clarity in which she decided enough was enough. It was as if a switch went off in her mind and she decided that she was too exhausted and disgusted by what she had to do to get the money to feed her habit to continue. At this point, many people self-destruct rather than make the arduous journey back to sobriety and a new way of being in the world. Schemel however phoned her father and shortly after went to stay with him while she joined a rehabilitation program. Part of Schemel's rehabilitation involved living in a women's 'sober house' and working as a dog groomer and walker at a nearby boarding facility. The dogs made her 'feel seen and needed and loved' and their faith in her helped her discover that she could be a responsible person. She began to like herself.[35]

No doubt Schemel's distress at being taken off the recording of *Celebrity Skin* was in part due to the crucial function that drumming played in her life. The moment after completing a set was a rare experience of peace for Schemel, and the drums symbolised the 'god of her own understanding'.[36] They helped her transcend her acute self-consciousness — so to be told she wasn't good enough to play them was like having the door to peace closed in her face. It's not surprising, therefore, that part of Schemel's turnaround involved picking up the drums again, not as an outlet for aggression or to feel powerful, but as a means of helping others along with herself: she became a drumming teacher for children. Like many recovering addicts, Schemel learnt of the joy that nurturing others can bring when you realise not everyone is out to hurt you — that you're worthy of love and of the effort to become clean.

The Equally Problematic Nature of Shame and Guilt

Some psychologists suggest that while shame can have harmful consequences, guilt benefits us in various ways and is less tied up with our self-concept.[37] They propose that guilt is associated with what we *do* while shame is related to beliefs about who we *are*. The psychoanalytic tradition, however, recognises that we're just as able to have a guilty self-concept as a shameful one. In other words, if we do something 'bad' we can indeed identify as *being* bad.

Researchers also point out that shame-prone people are generally less likely than guilt-prone people to think of how their actions might affect others.[38] Guilt can therefore seem like a more adaptive emotion than shame since it involves thinking about consequences. But for those who fit the bill for guilt-proneness, it's all too clear that life can be as taxing, painful and confusing as it is for the shame-prone person dealing with addiction (to power, fame, money or drugs). The presence of more acceptable behaviour in a guilt-prone person, though perhaps not causing issues for others, doesn't necessarily reflect a healthier inner life.

The self-denial, emotional containment and fear of calamity associated with guilt-proneness can severely limit our capacity for fulfilment, and can lead to a range of debilitating anxiety disorders. And while the guilt-prone person is less likely to engage in what we'd commonly regard as risky, impulsive behaviour, they too can 'act before they think' via their compulsive need to help others, thereby hurting themselves.

The guilt-prone person, like the shame-prone person, therefore pays a high price for their defences. Perhaps, for our purposes, remorse is a better term for what we feel when we have done something wrong and wish to make amends or do better in the future; remorse indicates that guilt hasn't become incorporated into our self-concept. Likewise, we can all feel embarrassed when we do something that makes others laugh at our expense, but embarrassment is not the same as shame: shame is more profoundly connected to who we believe we are.

In summary, though the words 'shame' and 'guilt' are sometimes used interchangeably, they do represent different emotional and psychological phenomena. Shame is based on feelings of inferiority and a fear of abandonment, while guilt relates to feeling 'bad' and is based on a fear of punishment. The shame-prone person fears their emotional dependency, while the guilt-prone person fears their personal power. Whether we identify more with shame or guilt will also guide our perceptions in every facet of life. The guilt-prone person will perceive hardship or unfortunate events as a form of punishment: 'Why does this always happen to me?' The shame-prone person is likely to perceive innocent remarks as derogatory: 'Are you laughing at me?' Whether we are operating under the influence of shame or guilt, we take things *very* personally.

We all experience shame and guilt, but for some of us the fear of abandonment is the leading source of discomfort with fear of punishment second, while for others the opposite is true. Which one becomes dominant in our experience relates to a combination of factors, a significant one being our early relationships to the primary authority figures in our lives. Table 1 summarises the defining aspects of shame and guilt.

TABLE 1. Main Differences Between Shame and Guilt

	SHAME	GUILT
CORE CONCERN	Am I *good enough*? Have I done a great thing?	Am I *good*? Have I done the right thing?
FEAR	Rejection, abandonment	Retribution, punishment
PRIMARY NEED	Recognition, power	Safety, approval
ANXIETY AVOIDANCE	Self-inflation, aggressive dominance	Self-sabotage, suffering, compliance

4

Avoiding Shame and Guilt

The aggressive and compliant solutions involve a degree of emotional upheaval because they are based on fulfilling strong emotional needs – when these needs are met, we feel great; when they're not we feel terrible. To avoid this emotional turbulence, some people decide that it's best not to want much from anyone or from life generally. Horney refers to this strategy as the detached solution.

The Detached Solution

The detached type reasons that it's best to be free of needs that involve meaningful emotional engagement with others. Loving, fighting, dependency and competition are all things the detached person avoids. 'I don't care' is their mantra for dealing with conflict and many of us use this defence when things seem too complex, disturbing or challenging.

According to Horney, the detached person is likely to have felt overwhelmingly stifled in childhood. A compliant parent may have given affection but being close to them meant meeting their dependent needs for reassurance and emotional support – a demanding task for any child. Likewise, an aggressive parent's erratic temper and boundary violations would have made the idea of self-expression threatening.

In short, the detached solution stems from a 'damned if you do, damned if you don't' scenario: to reach for love meant being swamped by someone else's emotional needs, and to express individuality seemed dangerous. Rather than be pulled by one parent or pushed by the other, the detached type decides to withdraw from engagement altogether: they don't need love or to express themselves in any expansive way — they don't need much at all.

The minimising of personal needs and wishes is a significant component of detachment and one of its greatest casualties is our ability to feel connected to others. A need for understanding, the sharing of thoughts and experiences, a longing for affection, sympathy, and support, all fall by the wayside when we adopt the detached solution. We keep our pains and fears to ourselves and try to deal with them on our own.

Emily was a client who described many experiences that fit the bill for the detached solution. She recalled that as a small child she always had difficulty expressing what she wanted for her birthday. There were things that appealed to her but she didn't feel any great desire for them, nor could she bring herself to ask for them. She also remembered that on shopping trips with her mother she would say no to anything her mother suggested they buy, even if she wanted it. 'I don't need it', was her internal monologue. It always perplexed her that after arriving home she'd feel regret for not buying the items she had refused — *why* had she said no?

Another giveaway that Emily had adopted elements of the detached solution was her profound difficulty in crying. Now in her twenties, Emily couldn't remember a time beyond very early childhood in which she cried, nor was she able to *let* herself cry as an adult — as soon as painful emotions began to surface, she would literally swallow them down as if taking a pill, and they would be gone. Emily also had a strong need for privacy and solitude and often felt encroached upon in the presence of others. This reflects the detached person's greatest defensive need: to feel free.

Needs and Wishes: Freedom's Prohibition

Where the compliant person idealises love and the aggressive person idealises mastery, the detached person idealises freedom: they aim for self-sufficiency in all aspects of life and pride themselves on their ability to fly solo. Most of all, the detached person doesn't want to be *bothered* by anyone or anything. They can't stand people or convention placing expectations on them because it makes them feel corralled. It's important to them that they never have to rely on anyone or *owe* anyone anything because that might lead to expectations of reciprocation.

The narrator (or nameless Underground Man) in Dostoevsky's novel *Notes from Underground* is a prime example of the detached type. He is a clerk living in nineteenth-century Saint Petersburg who reasons that he's stayed true to himself and his intelligence by not chasing after money or love. However, it's his need for freedom from the expectations of others that is the real source of his detachment; a freedom that he believes preserves his individuality and is worth preserving at all costs:

> *But I repeat for the hundredth time, there is one case, one only, when man may consciously, purposely, desire what*

> *is injurious to himself.... simply in order to have the right to desire for himself even what is very stupid and not to be bound by an obligation to desire only what is sensible... for in any circumstances it preserves for us what is most precious and most important — that is, our personality, our individuality.*[39]

Hypersensitive to anything resembling coercion, the Underground Man would rather do something he knows is detrimental to himself than comply with the expectations (or sound advice) of others and lose his sense of freedom.

The detached person also tends to minimise their talents and capabilities and settle for less in the name of freedom. Horney notes that in her practice, clients with this solution often became frightened when met with the realisation of their gifts. They didn't want to feel compelled to use them or to experience the emotional engagement that could come from expressing them. Instead, they were more comfortable maintaining a cynical view of life. They might pursue mediocre jobs though capable of much more, always defending their choices by affirming that nothing is that important anyway.

The Intellect as a Defence

Wary of emotional engagement, the detached person prizes logic and reason and can appear cool and detached in circumstances that others would find troubling. Sir Arthur Conan Doyle's fictional detective *Sherlock Holmes* provides an example of this kind of detachment. Holmes is dispassionate as he surveys horrific crime scenes and maintains a high level of objectivity regardless of the circumstances: 'I am a brain, Watson. The rest of me is a mere appendix'.[40] As with the Underground Man, this provides Holmes with an onlooker's perspective of life, and while he can make astute observations about human nature and society, he generally isn't affected by these observations because of his emotional detachment.

The compliant person's pride is based on moral superiority, the aggressive person's on power and status, and the detached person regards their general disinterest as a sign of intellectual superiority — they have resigned from things because any thoughtful person would see that nothing is worth much time or effort to achieve, as concluded the Underground Man: 'You know the direct, legitimate fruit of consciousness is inertia, that is, the consciously sitting with the hands folded'.[41] The detached person might equate this stance with a spiritual outlook in which renunciation of worldly concerns is a step towards enlightenment, however the detached person's equanimity isn't peace — the inner conflicts are still there, idling in the background and making their presence felt through the defence of detachment.

And while the detached person regards their inertia and listlessness as a burden deep thinkers must bear, it is the check on their wishes and strivings that is sapping their vitality and hindering their sense of direction. It's therefore not so much that the detached person has reasoned their way out of doing things but that they have immobilised any spontaneous movement towards love or ambition. Nonetheless they often feel the conflicts buried within: at times they're aware of craving intimacy, but their shame-prone tendencies will stop them from seeking it. Likewise, any impulse to strike out at someone will be stifled by guilt. The presence of both dependent and aggressive tendencies, though largely immobilised, can mean that they feel ashamed when they don't 'fight back' for example, and guilty if they do. The detached type (like all of us) can therefore experience times when they can't act in an unconflicted or straight-forward way.

The dynamics of all three solutions — summarised in Table 2 — are active, to a lesser or greater extent, in all of us. Which one is at the forefront of our experience can change over time and with experience, but for the compliant type, fear of punishment ('guilt anxiety') is the leading source of discomfort with fear of abandonment ('shame anxiety') in the background, while the reverse is true for the aggressive type.

Ideally, we can adjust our behaviour to the differing demands of circumstance — we can for example be a follower or leader, more submissive or dominant, or withdraw, depending on what seems right at any given time. If we become fixed in a solution we compulsively seek affection and approval, or power and recognition, or freedom and detachment. It also means we'll have a habitual way of perceiving and interacting with authority figures, and of meeting the prospect of having authority ourselves.

TABLE 2. Horney's Solutions to the Basic Anxiety

	COMPLIANT	AGGRESSIVE	DETACHED
FEARS	Initiative, decisions, aggression, assertion, power. Fear of punishment.	Intimacy, ostracism, weakness, helplessness. Fear of abandonment.	Anger, intimacy, helplessness, being 'bothered' or depended on.
SHOULDS	Be caring, do the 'right' thing, please everyone, make others happy, be helpful.	Be 'number one', be strong, powerful, admired or feared	Be detached, self-sufficient, avoid emotional investment.
AUTHORITY ISSUES	Obedient, seeks approval, prefers to follow rather than lead.	Doesn't like being told what to do, breaks rules, likes to lead.	No need to please or attack, prefers to operate independently.

Self-Estrangement: The Outcome of Every Solution

I'll walk where my own nature would be leading:
It vexes me to choose another guide.[42]

Emily Bronte

In adopting a solution, aspects of our true self are denied to maintain a self-concept that is good and caring, or strong and powerful, or wise and self-contained. Acknowledging and accepting our innate personality is necessary for happiness and wellbeing. A solution might keep anxiety at bay in the short-run, but the resulting self-estrangement ultimately leads to feelings of emptiness, anxiety and depression. We can feel fragmented — that we're a collection of parts rather than a unified whole — and feel disconnected from ourselves and others. It's for reasons such as these that Carl Jung regarded embodying our personality as the central task of our life. What exactly constitutes the wholeness of personality will be discussed in the following chapters, however it is helpful to think of your personality as being the preferences, temperament, quirks and talents that are an innate part of who you are.

Keeping unlived aspects of yourself at bay because of shame and guilt also uses energy. As members of the LGBTQI community often attest, hiding a fundamental aspect of yourself can be exhausting. Likewise, fatigue, anxiety, depression and a sense of meaninglessness are unavoidable for anyone struggling to accept integral parts of their personality. In contrast, self-acceptance of long-neglected aspects of the self can be reinvigorating.

Teenagers often experience this boost to their sense of well-being as they discover their own interests and path and begin to embody who they are as an individual distinct from their parents. I'm reminded of a client who experienced this kind of relief when she began to wear clothes that felt right for her, rather than wearing those chosen by her mother. Until then, she felt conspicuous, extremely self-conscious and somewhat depressed whenever they went out in public. The irony is that her natural style was much more alternative and eye-catching than her mother's, yet when she began to wear what she wanted she didn't feel conspicuous at all. Feeling good about ourselves doesn't depend on constructing an ideal self-concept that appeals to others. Instead it stems from our acknowledgement, acceptance and appreciation of what is innately right for us.

If we don't have a solid sense of self, grounded in acceptance of our fundamental nature, we can compensate by clinging to things which *do* have a strong identity associated with them — groups based on strong ideologies, for example, nationalism, or fundamentalism in whatever shape or form. We can also try to ground our identity in an interest or hobby. This gives us something to hold on to — a sense of significance and meaning where otherwise we'd feel the fragmented and vague nature of our identity.

This role of an intense interest, ideology or group membership was noted by the aforementioned Underground Man in Dostoevsky's novel: being a prime example of the detached type, he lacks the luxury of an intense interest to mitigate the sense of meaninglessness associated with not being himself. The Underground Man wishes he had a simple pleasure, a focus to occupy his life and give it a semblance of meaning. In this he would at least have something onto which he could project a stable identity:

> *I knew a gentleman who prided himself all his life on being a connoisseur of Lafitte [French wine]. He considered this as his positive virtue, and never doubted himself. He died, not simply with a tranquil, but with a triumphant conscience, and he was quite right, too.*[43]

Such is the case for all of us when we don't really know who we are or what we relate to: this desire to have *something* to define us in a consistent, dependable way and give us a feeling of significance. We can envy the sense of meaning and excitement some people derive from a particular interest — if only we could care that much about something! These are the times in which we are most vulnerable to the lure of fanatical missions. During the identity crisis of adolescence, approaching mid-life or assimilating to a new culture, for example, we can find the sense of purpose, camaraderie and identity of a fundamentalist organisation intoxicating. In this state, instead of experiencing the pain of a lacklustre life without purpose, those with a mission feel alive with righteous resolve.

Loneliness

Being disconnected from parts of ourselves also contributes to loneliness — to a feeling of estrangement from something or someone we care about. Loneliness can settle on us in a crowd, or amongst a group of friends. We might not think of our experience as loneliness, but we can nonetheless feel that there's no place or person with whom we feel at home. Melanie Klein suggested that underneath a longing for connection with others is a desire to be truly seen and understood.[44] Not only do we long to connect with ourselves, we long for someone else to see past our defences to the self we truly are and to accept it, which is perhaps the greatest need behind every trip to a therapist.

Another source of loneliness is the profound sense of difference we experience when we identify with shame and guilt. When we feel shame, we think we are the *least*. When we feel guilt, we think we are the *worst*. It therefore stands to reason that the more we identify with shame and guilt, the more different and isolated we'll feel. For people experiencing severe psychological distress, their sense of disconnect from others is so great that they experience life as if behind a pane of glass. Psychiatrist Frieda Fromm-Reichmann called this kind of loneliness 'real' loneliness to distinguish it from the loneliness of not having company when you want it — the kind of loneliness you can talk about to others. In contrast, real loneliness is an incommunicable emotional experience and involves a fundamental disconnect from reality.[45]

The book *I Never Promised You a Rose Garden,* is an autobiographical account of one of Fromm-Reichmann's patients, Joanne Greenberg, and provides a clear example of the correlation between shame, guilt, real loneliness and mental illness. Joanne's past contained events that, according to her childhood reasoning, meant she was unlikeable, bad, fundamentally different, and that the world was hostile towards her. At the heart of her pain was the idea that she was responsible for the misery and suffering of others — that she was literally 'poison' — and that she was inferior.[46] Indeed, if you dig deep enough into anyone's distress, you're likely to encounter the thoughts 'I'm bad', 'I'm not good enough', and 'I'm alone'. For the person experiencing severe mental illness, these feelings come to the fore with an intense experience of not belonging in the world — something Joanne expressed as a difficulty in 'casting' with it.[47]

The suspicion that we are somehow fundamentally different from others is something we all experience at some stage during our development. On the one hand, we can revel in the idea that we are unique — that we have distinctive gifts, talents and experience — but a sense of specialness is a double-edged sword that can turn against us leading to feelings of isolation and exclusion. Believing there is no one like us can be a very lonely position. Unsurprisingly, Joanne's recovery ultimately involved the realisation and acceptance that she and the world were indeed 'made of the same substance' — that she wasn't bad/dangerous or inferior/unlovable, that the whole world wasn't out to reject or punish her, and that she did indeed *count*.

Through therapy she became aware of the sources behind her belief that she was fundamentally 'worse' and 'less' than everyone else. Of significance was a terrifying stint in hospital as a child during which her parents were encouraged to stay away, and a holiday at a summer camp for children where she was subjected to persistent anti-Semitic taunts. Incidents like these had led Joanne to decide she was inferior and 'damned'. This belief began to colour her entire perception of the world. For example, she began to interpret the love she received from her mother as pity in acknowledgement of her hopeless fate. Indeed, how we process distressing events matters as much as the events themselves; Joanne's interpretation of these events was at the heart of her suffering.

Conclusion

The dilemma we all face from the time we are born is how to get our security needs met while inching towards independence. These needs are reflected in our yearning to be recognised, cared about, and protected from harm. Ideally, our moves towards independence and self-expression aren't at the cost of our parents' support and love. However, even an 'ideal' upbringing can't prevent a child from feeling deprived, unfairly treated, and unworthy at times.

Because feeling seen and cared for by our primary caregivers is vital to our sense of security, we contrive a false self based on their expectations and on those of society and its institutions. Horney proposes that our need for security is *the* motivating factor behind our need for approval and affection on the one hand, and for recognition and power on the other; needs which become major driving forces towards certain goals.

Horney's solutions describe three ways of being that defend us from shame and guilt, however each of these place restrictions on our authentic self. In the compliant solution, self-expression is sacrificed for fear of retribution, in the aggressive solution intimacy is sacrificed for fear of abandonment and in the detached solution both the need for self-expression and intimacy are radically curtailed. While either one set of needs is sacrificed for another or both are heavily policed, the repressed needs remain and their presence means we can never wholeheartedly move towards anything — the opposing tendency always pulls at us, and this produces inner conflict. To experience wholeness is to be able to move freely in one direction in any given moment.

Whenever inner need or circumstance calls for the expression of a neglected aspect, the underlying conflict between what we are called to express and the demands of our solution will cause us anxiety. Often, feeling unable to cope with a situation isn't so much about the objective nature of the challenge or our true ability to deal with it, but with the danger we've associated with being assertive or vulnerable. Also, if we look through guilt-prone eyes we'll perceive difficulties as a sign of worse to come, while if we are shame-prone we're likely to perceive them as a threat to our sense of power. Not aware of the true nature of our inner conflict, we don't know why we feel so anxious and ill-equipped to deal with what's in front of us.

Furthermore, our most compulsive, repetitive and driven behaviour is aimed at protecting us from shame and guilt. In contrast to the wishes, feelings or interests of our true nature, our defensive needs have an 'I must, or else...' character to them. They elicit what psychologists refer to as 'cognitive fusion': an obsessive type of thinking with a narrow focus and strong problem-solving orientation. Being able to take a step back from our thoughts and simply observe them without judgement — to 'slow down and pan out' — is a step towards a 'defused' state of mind, but is best achieved once the shame and guilt behind our compulsions is acknowledged.

Horney suggests that one way of distinguishing a simple, uncontrived 'I want' of our true self from the 'I must, or else' of a solution is that a defensive need will often have us acting against our own best interest. We saw this with the Underground Man's assertion that he'd rather do something detrimental to himself rather than go along with the advice of others in order to protect his *freedom*. Likewise, some elite athletes drastically risk their health in order to gain a competitive advantage, undergoing experimental body-modification surgery or taking harmful drugs to satisfy their relentless drive to be the *best*. And some people would rather stretch themselves to the point of exhaustion, compulsively choosing again and again to fulfil the requests of others in order to gain *approval*.

Our many achievements can deceive us into thinking we are the captain of our ship. We believe we know what we want and what we are striving for, but so much of what we do is governed by unconscious motives which reflect self-estrangement and identification with shame and guilt. Part Two of *Above the Battleground* addresses our need to reverse self-estrangement. It also introduces the notion of a transcendent Self: Integration of our personality involves answering the question 'Who am I?' on a higher, 'spiritual', level — a process that is central to the second half of life.

Part Two

P.M.

5

Reclaiming the Self

Carl Jung divided the course of life into two halves, each with different orientations. According to this schema, our focus in the first half of life is predominantly external. As infants, we want to explore our surroundings; indeed, we need to focus on our environment and stimulate our senses to mature physically and mentally. We maintain a largely external orientation as we move through adolescence into adulthood in that we're heavily influenced by the expectations of society, peers, tradition, and authority figures.

Mid-life marks a turning point in orientation. Instead of looking outward for direction and meaning, we need to reorient our focus to our inner world and connect with the wholeness of our personality. Achieving this connection means relinquishing our solutions and addressing our shame and guilt. The security we thought we gained through our defences is then replaced with a true, stable sense of security grounded in wholeness.

No one could say that growing up is easy. Navigating our way through childhood, adolescence, and into adulthood is a notoriously rocky road on which the 'shoulds' and 'oughts' of others often conflict with our own aspirations. Balancing the need to be ourselves with our need for security means that the self we end up presenting to the world isn't entirely honest. We do things that don't really gel with us; we repress innate qualities and preferences that do. Although our discarded aspects are latent, they still demand to be noticed. Many of the behaviours and interests we developed in the first half of life and which helped establish a sense of identity may therefore need to be questioned around mid-life. It is at this time that the call of our unlived aspects is felt most acutely.

Recapping Part One, if we identify with shame more than guilt we'll fear rejection and ridicule more than punishment and seek to feel secure by accumulating power and significance. When we identify with guilt more than shame, we seek for security in being self-effacing and compliant. Alternatively, we might decide that the best strategy for security is to be self-sufficient by not investing emotionally in anyone or anything. All three strategies are manifested in strikingly different attitudes towards authority — both our own and that of others — and in the nature of our emotional neediness.

To reclaim our self, we need to switch from an outward focus to an inward one. Jung suggested that we can think of our personality as developing linearly in the first half of life — we *construct* a self as time goes by based largely on what the world tells us is meaningful and in reaction to outer pressures and experience. In contrast, Jung described mid-life as a period in which we begin to circle our innate self. What this means is that everything we do or aim for now needs to emerge from an inner necessity rather than from trying to think of what might make us happy or be good for us — ideas that are often unconsciously motivated by the security needs of our solutions. In the first half of life it's par for the course to do many things thinking they *should* make us happy. In the second half of life, however, the need to reorient to our heart rather than our head is more pronounced.

Reading the Signs

> *The search for truth is accompanied not by whoops of joy, but by a sense of agitation and foreboding.*[48]
>
> Blaise Pascal

Jung found that for real psychological transformation we periodically have to undergo a dark phase in which our self-concept is challenged. What this means is that the sense of security we derive from our various roles needs to be relinquished. If we have over-identified with our roles (which we all do to some degree), then we have become dependent on them for a sense of value and significance. The process of transformation can only begin when we are willing to look beyond our roles and external validation for our sense of identity and value.

Frustration, boredom and emptiness at mid-life can signal a need to let unexpressed aspects of our personality emerge. Things that we used to find meaningful might no longer satisfy us and we can feel stuck, not knowing why or what to do about it. Often, feeling stuck, we dream of stagnant water. The source of our difficulty is that we have reached a threshold of change — we have grown so much that we are ready for a significant internal shift, and this can involve contemplating external changes that cause anxiety.

While psychological and emotional growth generally occur incrementally, thresholds are places of radical inner change where we are challenged to move from our habitual ways and comfort zones to embody more of our personality. They therefore also require us to face our shame and guilt, and often elicit childhood issues. Old feelings of exclusion, victimisation or being 'second-best' can come to the fore, taking us by surprise. An inexplicable spike in our sensitivity and anger at family gatherings, for example, can indicate that we are on the threshold of major inner change and growth.

We can also develop excessive concern for our health — 'hypochondriasis' — a preoccupation with the thought that we have, or are developing, a serious illness though we have only mild symptoms or none at all. Melanie Klein suggested that a fear of punishment — 'persecutory anxiety' — based on guilt for our anger is the basis of hypochondriasis.[49] Expanding on this, major thresholds can present enough change and uncertainty to the guilt-prone person (who is generally fearful of punishment lying around the corner — *What's next?!*) to trigger a period of hypochondriasis. Whether through guilt about anger, or fear of impending doom because of change, we can internalise a general sense of threat to our wellbeing and develop excessive concern for our health.

Klein also suggested that a fear of persecution could lead to what we now call 'conversion disorders' — cases of physical dysfunction without any biological cause but instead have their root in anxiety.[50] In other words, anxiety has been 'converted' into physical symptoms. The symptoms typically relate to the nervous system, such as paralysis or problems with the senses such as temporary blindness or deafness.

Conversion paralysis was prominent during the nineteenth century, but today the most common form of conversion disorder is somatoform pain disorder — severe physical pain that emerges spontaneously and without physical cause. An intriguing aspect of somatoform pain is that it can occur in the most stoic of individuals: people who are not averse to pain generally and have a high pain threshold. These same people will describe somatoform pain as unbearable.

Interestingly, modern perspectives on pain perception lend weight to the possibility that persecutory anxiety contributes to somatoform pain. Contemporary neuroscience tells us that we experience pain *only* when the brain 'decides' there is a significant threat to our wellbeing, and this conclusion is based as much on our thoughts as on physical reality.[51] We can therefore experience significant pain even though there's no physical problem, if our brain concludes there is danger. The important point here is the link between perceived threat and pain.

Sadness can be another sign of emerging issues. Just as our anger can lead to fear of retribution and concern for our own welfare, it can also lead to concern for the welfare of the object of our anger. This was a major insight of Klein's and it related to the importance she placed on the role of ambivalence in relationships. Klein suggested that much of our distress as children comes from our ambivalence towards our parents — we both love them and hate them, and our issues surrounding this are projected onto our partners and other authority figures later in life. (Indeed, any relationship that achieves a degree of depth will contain this mixture of love and hate because of emotional neediness.)

Klein's theory explored this ambivalence in detail, and she suggested that at every major point of 'inner or outer pressure' (such as encountered in a new life situation or major stage of development) these issues will be revived, along with associated feelings and fears surrounding rejection/abandonment and punishment.[52] Not only will intense anger related to feeling overlooked and unfairly treated surface (every child's perception to some degree), we'll feel guilty and sad if we also feel love towards the targets of our rage: our anger not only leads to concern for our own welfare (fear of retribution) but to sadness and concern for its hurtful effect on whom we love.

This 'depressive position' (Klein's term) comes from a fear that our connection to someone we love has been damaged or lost because of our anger, and is also self-punitive. As painful as this position is however, it is actually a sign of growth because it means that we no longer see someone as all good or all bad — we are aware of both our anger and love towards one person, rather than splitting these feelings and allocating each to different people, as Beethoven did with his parents (his mother 'all good', his father 'all bad'). Healing involves being able to face our love of a hated person and our anger towards a loved one. As Klein pointed out, 'Balance depends upon some insight into the variety of our contradictory impulses and feelings and the capacity to come to terms with these inner conflicts'.[53]

What helps us move through the depressive position is to know that our love is stronger than our hate, and what helps with this is having enough faith in our own goodness and capacity for love. This is one reason why Freud emphasised the importance of transference in the therapeutic relationship — as a client begins to transfer their parental issues onto the therapist and the therapist responds without judgement, the client's essential 'goodness' is reflected back to them, and this is the most potent source of healing. The internalising of a 'good object', as Klein put it, is what really sets the healing process in motion and is a key factor in helping us face our shame and guilt, thereby facilitating integration of the whole personality. It is also important to let go of the childhood belief in our omnipotence and accept that our anger doesn't have the power to irredeemably hurt someone.

Since the depressive position goes hand-in-hand with our demand that we be Number One in a parent's life (hence the anger at feeling overlooked), relinquishing the need to be the 'special one' in their eyes also helps us move on. We need, in effect, to ween ourselves off our parents — on our demand that they always be there for us, make us feel valued or approve of us. And again, establishing our essential goodness — a self, free of shame and guilt — is what helps us do this. This in turn releases the energy that had been tied up in our sadness so we can direct it to other things.

However, if our guilt is excessive, the poignant sadness associated with concern for someone becomes what is more commonly regarded as 'clinical depression' in which the focus is on our guilt and perceived unworthiness.[54] In his paper *Mourning and Melancholia,* Freud saw that the difference between normal mourning and clinical depression is that a person suffering from the latter 'displays something else besides which is lacking in normal mourning — an extraordinary diminution in his self-regard'.[55] Freud saw that the loss of a loved one provided fertile ground for our ambivalence to come to the fore:

> *The loss of a love-object is an excellent opportunity for the ambivalence in love-relationships to make itself effective and come into the open... In melancholia, the occasions which give rise to the illness extend for the most part beyond the clear case of a loss of death, and include all those situations of being slighted, neglected or disappointed, which can import opposed feelings of love and hate into the relationship or reinforce an already existing ambivalence.*[56]

In light of Klein's theory, if our feelings of anger are foremost, we might experience hypochondriasis, somatoform pain (or another conversion disorder) as a result of persecutory anxiety. If we become aware of both our love and anger, then we may experience sadness and remorse in the normal course of mourning, however if our guilt becomes excessive (for example, we find ourselves fused to thoughts of how we could have done more for someone, or been kinder), we will head down the road of depression and a one-sided, negative (and unfounded) view of ourselves.

Whether we have adopted the compliant, aggressive or detached solution, we can't cross a significant growth threshold without a direct conversation with guilt and shame. Like setting off on an expedition without a map or compass, if we don't know the larger context of our experience we can get lost in it and expend significant effort going down paths that lead nowhere. If we don't see our malaise for what it is, we can fall prey to well-meaning advice to simply find an activity we enjoy, become a volunteer, exercise more, go on a holiday, or slow down (or speed up!). All of these things have their place, but when it comes to major thresholds they rarely make a dent in our distress. Instead of making us feel better, such suggestions can make us feel misunderstood and isolated.

There is only one way out of our pain and that is to work through it. We need to understand that our unease is an indication that we have outgrown our former life and we are at a threshold of significant inner change — that there are aspects of ourselves that need to be acknowledged and developed. This involves allowing ourselves to enter into a period of darkness, confusion and instability as our grievances re-emerge and we begin to question our lives, values and self-concept. Allowing yourself to enter into the darkness is like letting yourself hit the bottom of the swimming pool so you can push yourself back up to the surface. It's not failure to allow yourself to meet your fear and distress: it's the most efficient way to stop struggling for air.

Inescapable Circumstances

Because facing the greatest sources of hurt and fear that underlie our shame, guilt and the adoption of our solution is painful, only a deep inner need or inescapable circumstances – such as losing a job, our home or a loved one – will cause them to surface. The aggressive person might be challenged to confront their fear of helplessness, while the compliant person might face their fear of putting themselves out there in some way (even if that means by taking a stance and saying 'no'). It also seems that – though we experience challenges in all areas of life – some people's external challenges tend to revolve around intimate fulfilment (namely finding the right long-term partner for example) while their work-life is relatively steady; for others the exact opposite is true.

Regardless of whether it is a relationship or a work situation we have outgrown, an increasing awareness that things need to change can be met with significant fear and resistance. We're likely to experience depression, anxiety and instability as things we've valued (financial security, a career, a relationship, our health) seem to be taken away from us, and old, painful issues with our parents emerge once again. This is the meaning behind the Jungian aphorism 'There's no growth without sacrifice': we will feel loss associated with an aspect of life we leave behind in order to go forward. The idea that inner conflict precedes growth can be helpful to remember in such circumstances.

Dr Elizabeth Kubler-Ross's five-stage theory on coming to terms with the inevitable nature of a significant loss or trauma (such as the death of a loved one, losing a job, or divorce) describes what the process of moving through resistance to change might look like. At first, we're likely to deny the problem, then become angry, envious or resentful (It's not fair!), then bargain (If I work harder, or change my attitude I won't have to find a new career/have surgery/get a divorce). After a period of time, however, we become resigned to the fact that change is inevitable, and this eventually leads to acceptance if we see our circumstances as a means for growth rather than an obstacle to happiness. Once this occurs, we've crossed a significant threshold, making room within ourselves to change through the experience.

The value of understanding that external trials are unavoidable in this world — that they are in fact our 'classroom' for transformation — is that we're less prone to judge our circumstances and ourselves. It challenges the idea that we attract difficulties or good fortune by our negative or positive thinking, a dangerous notion that actually compounds shame and guilt for those down on their luck and promotes a sense of moral superiority for others enjoying good fortune.

The idea that life operates according to a moral economy whereby fortune favours the good (or the positive thinker) inevitably creates a projection of guilt outwards and a search for scapegoats when times get tough. Periods of economic recession in medieval Europe, for example, have been linked to spikes in witchcraft trials.[57] People's unconscious guilt suggested hard times were their just reward, and so they projected their guilt onto (alleged) witches, blaming and punishing them for the recession. The Calvinist theology of the seventeenth century, which viewed worldly success as a sign of special blessing from God, also reflects the 'moral economy' idea.

It's much kinder to ourselves and others to focus on the *purpose* of our actions rather than their results since, as the Stoic philosopher Seneca said, that is the only thing we can control: 'And finally, the wise man regards the reason for all his actions, but not the results. The beginning is in our own power; fortune decides the issue, but I do not allow her to pass sentence upon myself'.[58] According to the Stoics, to live under the illusion that we have total control over externals such as our body, wealth or reputation is setting ourselves up for disappointment: anything external is vulnerable to the whims of fortune, and 'fortune gives us nothing which we can really own'.[59]

Though the process of coming to terms with our deepest fears associated with our self-concept can be extremely challenging, we are assured by myths which reflect common psychological and emotional processes that the end more than justifies the means. Mythologist Joseph Campbell, for example, developed a 'monomyth' called *The Hero's Journey* – 'one composite adventure… of the destiny of Everyman'[60] – based on his observation that ancient myths from many cultures symbolically depict this difficult process.

The monomyth involves the quest to live out the unlived aspects of our personality which are symbolised by a lost treasure. The call to adventure in myths usually comes via a dark or terrifying creature as judged by the world.[61] This reflects the fact that major thresholds of change often take on a frightening form

— events that don't usually give us a positive sense of adventure — and for this reason the journey rarely begins without some reluctance. We can ignore the signs that something needs to change or that our approach to life isn't working, however we're likely to increasingly feel that life lacks meaning and colour. Signs that something needs to give will become stronger until the call to adventure can no longer be denied.[62]

In myths, the hero confronts several dragons along their journey. The dragons represent the dictates of society and of our solutions that have stifled the expression of our truest self: the 'shoulds' and 'oughts' along with the shame, guilt and grievances associated with them. The dragons also represent the fear of looking at our issues. Because confronting dragons is no small feat, we need some help along the way, and we are assured by Campbell that this will be the case. In myths, help is often symbolised by the hero finding a protective amulet or meeting some kind of supernatural helper. In our own lives we might be supported by events that guide us: a book we find; a person we meet — such chance encounters can spur us on.

Upon finding and retrieving the treasure, the hero begins their return, often by surfacing from a subterranean environment into daylight. The precious object they acquire brings a boon to their community, and this reflects the fact that when we embody the wholeness of our personality, we not only benefit ourselves but can engage with others in a way that is a gift to them as well. With our newfound sense of self-acceptance and contentment, all the positive force we felt lacking before reappears along with a sense of possibility as we leave the past behind.

Another common metaphor for this process is 'The Night Sea Journey' of the sun. Just as the sun sets in the west and undergoes a night journey into the dark depths of the sea so it can re-emerge anew in the east, we have to pass through a period of darkness where we face our fears so we can meet the world from a different perspective.

A Declaration of Independence

Moving into our sense of wholeness involves extending our learning beyond what we have been taught by our parents, teachers, mentors or other significant authority figures. Artists for example often emulate the work of a master to help them learn their craft, but to truly allow for the flow of creativity they must cast an eye over what they have learnt and determine what's right for them and what isn't. In other words, they must find their own way — their own voice.

Thresholds of major change involve some form of growth in our own authority, and this can mean going down a path that is different from that of our parents. Mozart broke with his father's approach and became a freelance musician and composer for a time, much to his father's disapproval. Likewise, Carl Jung had a life-changing falling out with Sigmund Freud when Jung (Freud's appointed 'heir') began to develop his own (conflicting) theories. The father–son dynamic was something both men were aware of and eventually led to their split. In a letter to Freud, Jung complained that he treated his followers as 'sons' rather than equals. Jung wanted to have collaborative discussions with Freud about their differences; Freud wouldn't have it. He couldn't regard Jung as anything but a son and himself a father. He therefore interpreted Jung's difference of opinion as rebellion and wouldn't engage in a productive dialogue. Freud didn't want to give up his superior position, and so Jung had to go his own way.

Jung was thirty-eight years old when his ten-year friendship with Freud came to end with much residual bitterness. It was a profound break and led to an inner crisis and many prolonged depressive experiences between 1912 and 1919. Jung had left Freud's fold but hadn't yet fully developed his own theory: he felt adrift with no secure foundation.[63] To fully process the depths of his inner process Jung left his secure and prestigious job as a lecturer at university. This move along with his break from Freud left him feeling isolated: the majority of his friends had turned away, and a book he had recently published wasn't well received. Feelings of uncertainty, disorientation, anxiety and depression were accompanied by bouts of insomnia and stomach complaints.

The loss of friendships, a steady job and prestige were the sacrifice Jung experienced in order to probe the depths of his fears and find his own way. The eventual product of his Night Sea Journey was a wealth of new psychological insights that formed the basis for his own analytical psychology and a book on psychological types that has had a huge influence on psychological theory. Likewise, it's not uncommon for us to experience a very unsettling period as we move away from a family business or into a field that our parents have no appreciation for — perhaps even counsel us against — later to experience recognition and appreciation from an entirely different audience.

Relationship Trouble and the Laws of Attraction

Being authentic, or not coming from the dictates of our solution, isn't simply a matter of acting on impulse. The Surrealist art movement of the 1920s exemplifies this kind of misunderstanding. Surrealism was heavily influenced by Freud's theories on repression and the unconscious — Surrealists wanted to liberate our true desires from the dominance of reason and social conventions. Psychic Automatism was a technique they put forward for accomplishing this kind of liberation through art. It involved working extremely fast so as to bypass any inner censorship, thereby (supposedly) reflecting the repressed contents of the mind.

The problem with Psychic Automatism is that it doesn't take into account our resistance to repressed, unconscious material coming into the open. We can't just decide to 'let it out'. Instead, our unconscious conflicts are expressed in more enigmatic ways such as slips of the tongue or consistently forgetting someone's name. We also project our inner world onto the outer, which is the reasoning behind the famous Rorschach ink test — different people will interpret fairly abstract images differently according to the dynamics of their inner world and beliefs. Likewise, one of the best ways to know ourselves is to look at the way we perceive others — at what repels us and what attracts us.

Whether or not we consciously subscribe to the romantic idea of completion through union with someone else, an unconscious search for completion is a major factor in why we find certain people attractive — in them we see positive aspects of ourselves that we have repressed; they represent the untapped potential in ourselves. Jung used the term 'opposite containment' for a relationship in which a partner is chosen so they can be the 'container' for the parts of our personality we have repressed.

The compliant person for example might admire the self-confidence of an aggressive person; an aggressive person might be attracted to the warmth and discipline of a compliant type. Once the honeymoon period is over, however, and we don't feel our emotional needs (the defensive needs of our solutions) are being met, all we seem to see in our partner is the negative aspect of what was once admired: confidence appears as arrogance, assertiveness as aggression, bravery as foolhardiness, and spontaneity as impulsiveness. Likewise, the warmth we were attracted to can seem clingy and dependent, and conscientiousness can seem like fussiness.

A relationship of opposite containment therefore becomes one of conflict and tension as one partner habitually adopts self-negation and compliance, and the other adopts aggression and dominance. While couples can maintain this kind of dynamic for many years, there comes a point when irritation becomes acute and may be accompanied by significant anxiety and/or depression. This often occurs around mid-life when the call of repressed aspects intensifies — we simply don't want to remain within the confines of our solution anymore.

Unlike what we might assume, this doesn't necessarily signal that a relationship is wrong for the individuals involved. Relationships tend to go through a crisis before each person becomes more of themselves. The call of our repressed aspects cause us anxiety (because we decided long ago that they couldn't keep us safe), and parental issues of abandonment and punishment will surface (as they do at major thresholds of inner change). We project our parental issues onto our partner, responding to them in the same way we responded to a parent, and unconsciously expecting them to behave as a parent did. This primes us to perceive situations in a way that confirms our past learning and expectations.

Relationships provide fertile ground for misunderstandings because we can't hear or understand someone else when we are coming from our defensive needs, and whenever the defensive needs of our solutions aren't met, we will feel victimised. This was the case for Tom, a man in his late thirties experiencing severe anxiety at the prospect of his partner, Peter, undergoing treatment for cancer. The main source of Tom's anxiety was the change he was anticipating in Peter's mood and attitude towards him. Peter had not been an easy patient when ill in the past. He was uncompromising when it came to disagreements about how things should be done and was generally irritable. Tom had many of the traits of a guilt-prone or compliant person. He was a perfectionist, felt compelled to ease the suffering of others and had a strong need to please. Peter on the other hand, was a classic aggressive type. We can understand Tom's apprehension at dealing with an increase in his partner's antagonism — difficult patients aren't easy to cope with. But the extent of Tom's anxiety showed that the situation was some sort of 'button' for him.

Ultimately, Tom couldn't face the discomfort he felt when someone was upset with him — as it often seemed when Peter was sick and more argumentative than usual. Also, his efforts at being helpful needed to be rewarded with affirmations of his goodness. Peter's responses, however, suggested to him that much of what he did was wrong. For Peter, sickness and the dependency it brought was a sign of weakness — anything suggesting helplessness is the most poignant dread of the aggressive type, and in times of stress our defences become more pronounced. As Peter's antagonism grew, Tom's need to please him increased. In such situations at least one person needs to be willing to see that the other's 'offensive' behaviour stems from fear, as does their own distress.

When two people are operating from their solutions, there is no real 'relating' going on — at least not with each other. Trying to fulfil the unmet security needs of childhood means we are unconsciously relating to someone in the present as if they were a figure from our past, which was the case for Tom with Peter. We are often attracted to partners who turn out to have the qualities of a parent we had problems with — someone whom we hold responsible for causing us the most pain in life. Our partner can then serve as a screen onto which we project a harsh, punitive or emotionally absent parent.

Thus, when two people are reliving their past by projecting it onto the present, they are inhabiting psychically separate, private worlds and are apt to feel alone. They are also prone to attack each other whenever their past hurts are activated, in retaliation for the past, hitting out at someone who isn't there. When we are coming from our solutions, we are therefore egocentric — consumed with our needs because of our insecurity, making it difficult to consider anyone else's position. This lack of real communication and understanding is one reason our relationships can seem impersonal after a while and we become lonely, bored or apathetic towards our partner.

Though relationships based on opposite containment can be difficult, they can provide significant opportunities for growth because our judgements of differences illuminate what we have deemed unacceptable in our self. They can thus be utilised as a means of growing into an independent sense of wholeness. Conversely, for some couples who are poles apart in terms of solutions, the conflict in a relationship based on opposite containment can prove to be too great, painful and indeed unhelpful (particularly if it becomes abusive), and so the relationship ends. It's not uncommon to then seek out someone we are more 'compatible' with — someone who is more like ourselves.

Jung called this second type of relationship 'defensive containment'. In these relationships, it's the sameness that attracts each partner — both partners have the same unconscious fears and solutions. This doesn't mean that there won't be arguments. Relationships between aggressive types for example can be volatile, erratic affairs. They don't however have the kind of conflict that challenges their solutions — there is no pressure to change.

Likewise, if one person in a partnership based on defensive (or opposite) containment feels the urge to move beyond their solution but the other isn't agreeable to this, conflict usually ensues. Such a scenario is at the heart of Richard Yates' novel *Revolutionary Road.* Set in 1955, the novel focuses on Frank and April Wheeler, a couple who have chosen the well-trodden path of marriage, two children, a good job and a nice house in a conventional American suburb. When Frank and April first meet, they are full of idealism about having a fulfilling, adventurous life, but when April becomes pregnant and she and Frank buy a house in the suburbs, they find themselves slipping into the kind of pre-fabricated existence they once despised. Frank ends up in a job he hates, working for the same company his father worked at for twenty years, and April — who had studied acting and aspired to be an actress — becomes a stay-at-home mother who endures all the stifling expectations that go along with this role in the 1950s.

There is a seductive pay-off to this kind of existence: it is safe, secure and predictable. Still, the price that Frank and April pay for their safe life is high. They have the security of a steady income and a home, but their unlived aspirations impose a sense of alienation and claustrophobia. As both characters refuse to be honest with themselves about the source of their frustration, they project it onto each other and argue. In the end, April's growing awareness that she needs things to be different clashes with Frank's fear of sacrificing security and she retreats from the world by becoming numb to it, mechanically fulfilling her role with a facade of pleasant equanimity. No longer does she discuss her longings and emotional experience with Frank. She sets out to manage her existence on her own, keeping her despair to herself, and eventually makes a decision that has catastrophic consequences.

Indeed, a longstanding and characteristically 'mellow' relationship based on defensive containment can therefore become full of conflict around mid-life when a person feels the call of their repressed opposite but is discouraged from exploring this by their partner. They might then seek out a relationship based on opposite containment, being attracted to the unlived (but desired) aspects of themselves seen in another. And so it goes, perhaps for the rest of our lives, as we seek to either complement or defend our habitual behaviours in order to obtain a sense of wholeness or security that can only be realised within. As we'll see in the following section, a significant obstacle to such realisation is the idea that certain attributes are fundamentally linked to gender.

Mars and Venus

Psychologists refer to a tendency to see things in a polarised way as 'black and white thinking'. You might, for instance, view some people (including yourself) as all good or all bad. Though black and white thinking isn't good for us (it's been linked to chronic anxiety amongst other things) there seems to be a profound human tendency to engage in it, particularly in relation to gender.

Horney's compliant and aggressive solutions resemble male and female stereotypes. This isn't surprising considering historical religious and societal influences regarding what constitutes 'normal' behaviours, preferences, and talents according to our biological sex. In the late nineteenth century, Professor Edward Clarke of Harvard University wrote in his treatise *Sex in Education* that if a woman studied excessively, blood would be diverted away from the uterus to the brain, thereby causing irritability and infertility. Likewise, it has been assumed that men as a whole have a psychological and emotional constitution suitable for conscription into the armed services.

Though we question such assumptions today, the attempt to reinforce gender-roles by establishing a biological basis for them continues. Clinical neuroscientist Cordelia Fine, for example, points out in her book *Delusions of Gender* how modern neuroscience is being used to reinforce old-fashioned stereotypes by claiming there are 'hard-wired' differences between the brains of men and women that make them fitted for different roles. For those intent on maintaining that there is more that separates the sexes than unites them, the idea of the brain as an isolated processor unaffected by experience such as socialisation is very appealing. The truth is more complex. Contemporary understanding shows that what we learn and how we think can all change neural structure directly. As Fine concludes, the fact that experiences change the brain seems to make the word 'hardwiring' redundant.[64]

Stereotypes are however very hard to shift. We tend to associate men with action, strength, self-belief, and independence; women with caring, tenderness, goodness, thoughtfulness, self-sacrifice, and nurture. Such assumptions have far-reaching effects. For example, in a recent study by Jodie Waisberg and Stewart Page, clinicians' diagnoses of patients were related to the degree that symptoms deviated from gender role stereotypes.[65] Female patients with 'masculine' symptoms (e.g., alcoholism or antisocial behaviour) were seen as more psychologically disturbed than males with the same symptoms, and male patients with 'feminine' symptoms (e.g., depression and anxiety) were seen as more psychologically disturbed than their female counterparts.

Unfortunately, much of what is touted as 'relationship coaching' still revolves around the idea that men and women are profoundly different in terms of their psychological and emotional makeup, needs and capabilities. John Gray's hugely popular *Men Are from Mars, Women Are from Venus* tells us that men and women should maintain 'complementary' roles. Men like to do, provide and decide. Women like to be adored. *That* old chestnut! The tools given in books such as Gray's are really about playing to the defensive needs of the shame and guilt-prone types. This is why Gray's advice is so counterproductive — it distorts our perceptions of neurotic extremes by binding them to gender. As Horney puts it, 'self-effacement has nothing to do with femininity, nor aggressive arrogance with masculinity. Both are exquisitely neurotic phenomena'.[66]

That men and women have both masculine and feminine characteristics is central to Jung's analytical psychology, which views integration of these aspects as fundamental for our wellbeing. It's unfortunate that we have dichotomised just about everything in terms of gender. I don't believe that things such as logic and reason are inherently 'male', nor emotion and intuition inherently 'female'. However, the fact that these qualities have been labelled as such means coming to terms with what is 'feminine' or 'masculine' within us.

Our relationship to what is masculine and feminine within and without is also strongly influenced by our earliest relationship with our parents. Not having felt loved or supported enough by a parent, we can develop contempt for their gender as a whole along with the masculine or feminine within ourselves. Just as we feel deprived and persecuted by a parent, we can project that out and feel the same towards the entirety of their sex, somehow feeling impoverished or persecuted by men or women generally.

Recalling the discussion of John Bowlby's attachment styles from Chapter Three, this sort of projection involves acting out an 'ambivalent' attachment, one in which we strike out at those we feel have abandoned or rejected us. Hatred (in the form of misogyny and misandry for example) is still a form of attachment because we can't hate someone unless we feel our happiness depends on them in some way and that they have deprived us of it. What we really hate is our dependency, exposed by our vulnerability to how others treat us and those with whom we identify. This is why each of us experiences a love-hate relationship with our primary caregivers or those we depend on for love and security: we love them for the approval, security and warmth they give us but hate them for exposing our (shameful) dependence and vulnerability.

In summary, embodying our personality isn't simply a matter of being ourselves. It often involves facing difficult circumstances, the loss of friendships, conflict with partners, and going against the tide of expectations and approval. It's a route that many people avoid by focusing on the outer world and its distractions.

If, however, we intuit what it would be like to embrace our whole self, the disparity between what *is* and what *could be* becomes intolerable — the pain of identifying with shame and guilt outweighs the fear of facing the insecurities associated with them. What adds to the difficulty of this process is that our shame, guilt and authority problems not only relate to our personal history but — as we'll see in the following chapter — to our unconscious associations regarding a Divine Authority as well.

6

Beyond the Personal

As mentioned in the previous chapter, Freud and Jung's friendship turned sour when their theories began to conflict. In particular, they differed in their assumptions about the unconscious. Freud viewed it as a reservoir of the forgotten and the repressed, along with self-preserving (sexual) and destructive (aggressive) 'instinctual' drives. Jung, on the other hand, believed there was a deeper layer of the unconscious containing all that is 'prophetic and eternal'.[67] To Jung, this deeper layer possessed a wisdom concerned with moving us towards embodying our wholeness.

The Collective Unconscious

Jung's clientele differed greatly from Freud's. Freud worked with private 'neurotic' patients who maintained contact with reality because the once-repressed contents of their unconscious came through in a measured, containable way — indeed, making the unconscious conscious was a challenge for Freud's patients. In contrast, Jung worked with hospitalised psychotic patients who had lost contact with reality — who were *swamped* by the contents of their unconscious and the conflicts within it.

Jung was struck by the delusions of his patients because they often contained symbols from myths and religions that couldn't have been known to them. He also observed that the narratives of many myths from across time and culture paralleled the psychological processes of his patients. To account for this, Jung suggested that our minds inherit common symbols and themes from the larger cumulative experience of humanity. He called this common psychological inheritance the collective unconscious, the contents of which are identical in all of us. For Jung, the personal unconscious rests on the deeper layer of the collective unconscious.

The collective unconscious can be thought of as the myth-creating level of mind. Myths are a way of ordering and making sense of our experience. They are stories containing themes and images that represent major psychological processes, and common elements can be found across time and place. Jung gave the name 'archetypes' to such universal content of the psyche. A major implication of the theory of archetypes is that we are born with a kind of blueprint for approaching, perceiving and interpreting typical major life events (such as birth, separation, marriage, and death). Archetypes relate to the most meaningful processes of emotional, psychological and spiritual growth. The universal figure of the Hermit for example is an archetype that represents the common call to retreat at times from external distractions in order to reconnect with our inner world.

Of particular relevance to our discussion of shame, guilt and the 'basic conflict', are the archetypes of Mother and Father. These archetypes represent aspects of the parent-child relationship that have left an indelible imprint in the collective unconscious of humanity — the most potent aspect relating to the tension between our desire for self-expression and our dependency, between the need for freedom and security, leading to fears of abandonment and punishment. This means that we are born with a prototype of the 'basic conflict' active in our minds, organising our perception according to this theme.

The large amount of conflict associated with the Mother and Father archetypes is surpassed only by one other — the archetype of God. The God archetype reflects our predisposition to believe in an overarching power of creation. Even if we identify as atheist, the God archetype will be operating in our unconscious, influencing our perceptions and relationships with authority figures. Indeed, Jung proposed that because of the immense conflict associated with the God archetype, we repress it and project our 'God-related' issues onto our parents. Thus, our perceptions of God and our parents are intertwined.

The Mother and Father archetypes are representative of the two aspects of God — love as well as will, nurture as well as direction. When we feel deprived of these from our parents, the archaic, archetypal force behind the theme at hand increases the emotional intensity of our experience. Or, to put it another way, when we (unconsciously) feel unfairly treated by God, we will project our anger onto our parents and feel victimised by them, blowing the situation out of proportion.[68]

Jung and Freud agreed that the way we perceive our parents is linked to our ideas about God and that we are mostly unconscious of this association. Freud was of the opinion that man made God in the image of his parents, while Jung proposed the reverse. Either way, to understand how and why we perceive our parents as we do, it is helpful to consider some of humanity's recurring concepts about God.

The Fall

Independence versus dependency, power versus subservience, and freedom versus security are all forms of expressing the perilous dynamic between government and society, and parent and child. Surveying the myths of different cultures and times, this dynamic is also expressed in the relationship between God and 'His' creation.

An idea that occurs frequently in religious mythologies is that we once lived in peace and harmony with our Creator, but something happened to destroy this relationship, leading to feelings of abandonment, isolation, and suffering. A common theme in African mythology, for example, is that God was close to us but we upset Him, so He withdrew to a great distance.[69] In one story, the sky, where God dwells, was once much nearer to us — so close that it could be touched. Some women took bits of the sky to put in a soup and God became angry, retiring to his present distance, the sky retreating with him. In another myth from the Congo, God lived in the middle of Africa with his three sons and all were happy and content. Two of the sons disobeyed God and in retaliation He headed west with his obedient son, leaving the others in poverty and despair, vulnerable to decay and death.

The Biblical story of Adam and Eve is an iconic myth of the Western world, designed to explain our existential despair. It depicts an earthly paradise in which the first humans, Adam and Eve, lived in harmony with the rest of creation and were in close communication with God. The Garden was a place of abundance: Adam and Eve wanted for nothing, and even the *idea* of suffering was alien to them. Everything changed, however, when they disobeyed God and ate fruit from the Tree of Knowledge. With that one act of disobedience — of asserting an independent will — Adam and Eve's amicable relationship with God was destroyed. Furious at this violation of his sovereignty, God condemned Adam and Eve to live out their days in toil and suffering, adding death as a final blow — their disobedience disqualified them for immortality.

The theme of conflict between creator and created is a popular source of drama for plays, novels and movies. The enduring appeal of Mary Shelley's novel *Frankenstein* is a prime example of the prominence of this conflict within our minds. Written nearly two hundred years ago, *Frankenstein* is rediscovered by every generation because of its universal themes, which include the tragic consequences of playing God. Mary Shelley subtitled *Frankenstein* 'The Modern Prometheus', reflecting the Greek myth in which Prometheus stole fire from the god Zeus and gave it to mankind.

Since fire was the possession of the gods, to be given or withheld according to their choosing, Prometheus usurped their divine power. Zeus's retribution was to have Prometheus bound to a rock where an eagle would swoop down and eat his liver, which would continuously grow back so the torture could be repeated the following day. In *Frankenstein*, the doctor's ambition to create life by reanimating the dead had disastrous consequences, not least for himself. The message of such stories is clear — usurp the power of the gods at your peril.

Alienation is another prominent theme in *Frankenstein*. Just as Adam and Eve were expelled from the Garden of Eden — abandoned by God — Doctor Frankenstein abandons his responsibility as a parent and banishes his creature to a life of abject alienation and loneliness. The creature longs for companionship but everywhere is met with a hostile gaze, leading him to confront Frankenstein: *Why did you do this? Why did you create me, only to abandon me? Why don't you care about me?*

The idea of a fall from grace is prominent in myths because of our pain and suffering. Regardless of how good our external circumstances are, or how much money, fame or status we enjoy, none of us feel totally secure, loved or loving at all times. We all yearn for an elusive 'something else' and this begs the question: *can you miss something you've never had?* As the French philosopher and mathematician Blaise Pascal wrote: 'What else does this craving, and this helplessness, proclaim but that there was once in man a true happiness, of which all that now remains is the empty print and trace?'[70] Experiencing ourselves as distant from comfort and love, we feel abandoned and punished.

Following Jung's collective unconscious idea, these feelings and their relationship to an ultimate power or source, are an inherited part of our psyche — something present at birth, influencing our perceptions. The first godly figures we encounter are our parents; the first fall from oneness our birth, but the conflicts in our personal lives derive their potency as reflections of religious themes. We are therefore primed to perceive our world in accordance with the themes of punishment (for self-expression and initiative) and abandonment (for not being good enough).

While in the first half of life our issues are more consciously linked to our parents, the God archetype comes to the fore in the second half of life, albeit via parental issues. This presupposes that there is a developmental readiness for encountering the archetypes: while grievances relating to parental abandonment and punishment (and associated feelings of shame and guilt) are painful and challenging during the first half of life, they take on a new intensity in the second because of the emotional force of the God archetype behind them. They are more acutely felt, painful, and we can feel a sense of precariousness, instability, confusion, and disenchantment well above those of our early years, as difficult as they might have been.

And just as psychotic patients have strange symptoms when they are flooded with the unconscious (and the archetypes contained therein), people more grounded in reality but experiencing intense emotions (particularly at thresholds of change) can experience very strange symptoms as well. I recall a client from my therapeutic practice who was sure his pelvis would break apart every night as he lay in bed. Another going through a difficult transition feared that her head would fall off because her neck wasn't strong enough to carry it. She knew there was no real chance of this happening, yet her perceived experience made her fear otherwise — a fear of 'losing our head' is common during times of extreme inner turmoil.

That conflicts derive their potency from collective, existential themes is perhaps one reason many elite athletes suffer a profound sense of despair (even though they might have a surplus of money, fans and family support) when they are forced — by injury or otherwise — into retirement. As athletes, they are cared for, protected, nurtured, adored and have a strong sense of purpose. Their world is removed from the norm. When this 'Eden' is suddenly taken away from them they experience intense feelings of worthlessness, isolation, persecution (*What did I do wrong?*) and abandonment (*They use you then they spit you out and forget about you*).

Likewise, children who move from a country where they have friends and a sense of belonging can struggle significantly if their new home is unwelcoming and if their parents' relationship becomes strained — again there is the sense of a fall from security and comfort. Jung suggested that if a person couldn't get past an issue from their personal history, it was because it had the force of such an unconscious 'religious' association behind it.[71]

The Prodigal Son theme is another archetypal script that can play out through the first half of life. In it we find ourselves wasting our inheritance (money, education, a good upbringing) by heading down a path of self-destruction, folly or alienation, only to hit rock bottom and return, not (as we fear) to be met by judgement and rejection, but by love and acceptance. This theme has a redemptive quality and everyone has some version of the 'something lost, something found' theme expressed in their lives — everyone's fall is different in form, but it's a fall nonetheless.

Our lives follow a well-worn path in which a wounding in the first half of life becomes the means of returning to the comfort of our true, whole self in the second. Just as Hansel and Gretel dropped pieces of bread along their journey into the woods so they could find their way back home, our mistakes and grievances can light the path back to our self. As painful and disorientating as it is, working through our shame, guilt and authority problems — as we are called to do at thresholds of change — is what helps redirect our attention from the outer world to the inner. This reorientation not only leads to contacting our innate self but directs us towards communion with that which is eternal. Just as we have a deep-seated need or instinct towards embodying the wholeness of our personality, we have what Jung called a 'religious instinct', and this is explored in the following section.

Life is Absurd

> *There is no unhealthiness in divine discontent.*[72]
>
> J.A.C. Murray

The stress of the mid-life crisis doesn't just relate to the unintegrated aspects of our personality but to an existential crisis of meaning associated with growing old and the prospect of our mortality. In the first half of life we are met with a world of possibilities regarding where we might go, what career path to take, who we might meet; we imagine we have all the time in the world. In the second half of life, the inevitability of our death can't escape our awareness and we can feel like we're perpetually running out of time. For many people, the realisation that despite all of their accomplishments life will come to an end can make everything seem futile.

This was the case for the Russian author Leo Tolstoy, who at forty-one suffered a major depressive period that ushered in a ten-year inner crisis. Tolstoy had published two best-sellers, had literary fame, a large estate, a wife and fourteen children, yet he became steeped in melancholia at the thought of his mortality — for all that he had accomplished, what was it worth when everything, including himself, perishes in the end? Tolstoy gave a vivid account of this in his memoir, *A Confession*:

> *I could give no reasonable meaning to any single action or to my whole life. I was only surprised that I could have avoided understanding this from the very beginning — it has been so long known to all. Today or tomorrow sickness and death will come (they had come already) to those I love or to me; nothing will remain but stench and worms. Sooner or later*

> *my affairs, whatever they may be, will be forgotten, and I shall not exist. Then why go on making any effort? ... How can man fail to see this? And how go on living? That is what is surprising! One can only live while one is intoxicated with life; as soon as one is sober it is impossible not to see that it is all a mere fraud and a stupid fraud!*[73]
>
> *... My question — that which at the age of fifty brought me to the verge of suicide — was the simplest of questions, lying in the soul of every man from the foolish child to the wisest elder: it was a question without an answer to which one cannot live, as I had found by experience. It was: 'What will come of what I am doing today or shall do tomorrow? What will come of my whole life?'*
>
> *Differently expressed, the question is: 'Why should I live, why wish for anything, or do anything?' It can also be expressed thus: 'Is there any meaning in my life that the inevitable death awaiting me does not destroy?'*[74]

Tolstoy concluded that when we experience life as absurd, we need to have an explanation of it that connects the finite with the infinite in order to go on living. For him, the answer that gave life meaning was to forge a connection with God — not through church tradition or dogma, but through an inner experience — and that is what gave his life a sense of worth. Likewise, Jung wrote that the decisive question for all of us is whether we are related to something infinite or not: our greatest limitation is to believe we are only our finite self, and if we appreciate our link with the infinite our desires and attitudes will change.[75]

For Jung, a meaningful life is one in which we embody our innate character and make ourselves available to the guidance of our transcendent, spiritual Self — our wholeness is calling us to remember who we are on both a finite personality level, and an infinite, spiritual level. Indeed, Jung believed that many of our problems during mid-life belie a feeling of senselessness and aimlessness that can be relieved by developing a 'religious outlook'.[76] This has nothing to do with religion per se, but is based on a sense of mystery and appreciation of things unseen, not on the particular doctrines of a church. It's about assuming we are accompanied by something wiser and larger than our ego-self, and that there's more to life than the drive to 'become someone' or do something great.

A religious outlook reflects a reorientation from the outer to the inner, and a move from emphasising a rational apprehension of our world to an intuitive, more subjective one. In this sense, the shift in orientation between the first and second half of life recapitulates the historical shift from the Age of Reason in the seventeenth century into the Romantic Era toward the end of the eighteenth century. The Age of Reason marked a move away from superstition and the oppressive and fear-inducing ideologies of the Church — it was a coming of age necessary for people to start thinking critically and independently, which is a prerequisite for innovation. In the process of elevating scientific logic and reason however, mysticism and the poetic imagination of the intuitive self were undervalued. The Romantic Era introduced a reorientation to the inner world and an appreciation for what can't be seen or measured.

According to Jung, attempts to extend the priorities of the first half of life into the second indicate poor adjustment to the changing demands of the life-course. A focus on appearing forever young, for example, or on remaining fiercely competitive will only lead to despair and we're likely to ramp up the defining characteristics of our solution in a misguided attempt to regain the satisfaction we felt in the past.

Jung was unique amongst psychologists of his time for emphasising a relationship between embodying our personality and connecting with our spiritual Self.[77] This also had profound implications for those who believed in God but struggled with religious dogma that conflicted with their inner truth: Jung's theory meant that though listening to the call of our innate character might put us at odds with the creeds and injunctions of a religion, it isn't contrary to spiritual growth. Indeed, as we'll see in the next chapter, it is our Self that assists us in integrating the many facets of our personality.

A Tale of Two Selves

For many of us, the experience of peace and contentment that we gain from listening to music, meditation or reading something inspirational doesn't remain as we re-engage with the outer world. The outer world seems to be an impediment to the inner, but the problem is really one of dissociation — a split between our inner spiritual Self and our outer self that in later life calls for integration. This explains why Beethoven could produce deeply moving music from what must have been a loving place, and yet just as easily shout abuse at his housemaid for something trivial. And why Mozart, whose music is sublime, was yet plagued by a sense of emptiness at times.

Jung first came across the idea of an inner and outer personality during his childhood. As a small boy he felt he had two very different personalities which he called No.1 and No.2. No.1 was concerned with the outer world. It related to going to school, being interested in what he was learning, mucking about with his friends, feeling self-conscious, and performing his duties at home. No.2 related to his inner world and an altogether different experience of self: No.2 wasn't self-conscious, was connected to a timeless realm, and had an appreciation for the cosmos and nature.

Jung longed to be able to express his No.2 personality through No.1 and its connection with the outer world, but he knew he couldn't. When he was twelve years old, he had a dream that symbolised the need to first strengthen the outer ego-self before living from the abstract, spiritual centre. Jung dreamt that he was carrying a lamp with a small flame in it as he walked through a fierce storm. He fought hard to walk against the storm and knew he needed to protect the flame from going out. The flame represented his No.1 personality — the one concerned with the concrete nature of life, with intellectual learning and the capacity to understand things through logic and tangible experience. In the dream the flame cast a large, fearful shadow behind him, and this represented his No.2 personality. He had to keep his focus on not letting the flame blow out.

Jung interpreted this dream to mean that he must leave his No.2 self behind so that he could first find his anchor in the world — he needed to let the spiritual world of No.2 recede into the background and focus on the stuff of everyday living: he had to go to school, study, mess about with friends, make mistakes, and earn money.[78] He also knew that he mustn't totally forget his No.2 personality: he needed to let his No.1 personality come to the fore, but he recognised that No.2 was also an integral part of him and still needed to be acknowledged, *on the quiet*.[79]

It was around mid-life that Jung experienced a reawakening of his No.2 self which he was able to integrate into his external life via his professional writings. However, he couldn't have done this until he had built a psychological container in the form of a strong ego identity, forged by the trials and tribulations of engaging with the outer world.

The need to first 'cut our teeth' in the demanding and harsh external world before our spiritual nature can be adequately and safely expressed is the subject of a Navajo myth in which twin brothers go in search of their father, whom they have never seen.[80] When they finally find their father's house and enter, they are seized by him and hurled across the room into spikes. The father then tries to steam them to death in his sweat lodge. The trials continue but the twins survive. Eventually, the father is reassured by the twins' endurance that they are ready to be accepted into his house — to behold him as their father.

This dramatic picture reflects our need to first forge our identity in the world (symbolised by the trials the twins endure) before focussing on embodying our spiritual nature: that we need to be properly 'initiated'. This is because the depths of the spiritual world are both a source of joy and terror to us; not because there is anything negative about the abstract nature of our spiritual Self, but because of our deep-seated shame and guilt that obscure it. We need to develop a certain degree of ego-strength (capacity to function in the world) before attempting to face our bedrock shame and guilt — which will inevitably surface — as we move towards reconciling our No.1 and No.2 personalities. It means that before we can move beyond identification with our ego-self, we first need to have a solid sense of that self. This is why the rigorous mind-training exercises of Zen, for example, which are designed to lessen our sense of 'I' aren't intended for people who don't feel grounded in the physical world.

The need to respect our fear and allow ourselves to move slowly towards integration was illustrated in a dream I had in which I was walking down a hallway and stopped to look through an open door. Inside the room was a young girl sitting cross-legged on the floor, holding a deck of Tarot cards. She selected two cards and started to interpret them. I knew her interpretation was correct — that she was in tune with something — and as she realised this herself, she became very anxious. I suggested that she have a break from the cards and do some mathematics instead; I knew this would ease her anxiety. The dream represented my fear of my spiritual nature — though getting more 'in tune' with it would bring me joy, I also needed to appreciate my fear and move slowly, turning to the lighter, purely intellectual aspects of the tangible world ('mathematics') for respite.

Wholeness

The integration of our inner and outer personalities is one example of reconciling opposites — a process central to Jung's concept of wholeness which was influenced by Eastern philosophies and their emphasis on the interplay of opposites. In the Chinese Taoist creation myth for example, a world of opposites (yin/yang, female/male, black/white) emerges from a chaotic, formless void. This is clearly evident in the world — opposites abound — and in traditional Chinese medicine, maintaining a balance between the complementary elements of yin and yang maintains health and wellbeing. Likewise, Jung's idea of a whole personality was one in which our opposite characteristics are accepted and we allow ourselves to move between them as needed — to be assertive in some circumstances and compliant in others for example.

Notably, Jung's theory assumes that along with complementary functions such as thinking and feeling, our personality contains both 'good' and 'bad', 'light' and 'dark', and that both are necessary components of wholeness. In this respect Jung was in line with Freud's theory that aggressiveness and selfishness are 'natural' aspects of human nature, and that the best we can do is channel these dark drives in socially acceptable ways, such as through sport or artistic expression.

Horney also recognised that opposite functions such as thinking and feeling are complementary aspects of the personality, but she disagreed with Jung's theory that aggression or other 'dark' impulses are a part of wholeness. Instead, she regarded them as symptoms of an underlying conflict. As discussed in Part One, this conflict involves shame, guilt and the fears of abandonment and retribution. Horney's view on the embodiment of wholeness considers the *irreconcilable* nature of what is 'good' in us, and what is 'bad' — she maintains that only one reflects what is *true* about us. This being the case, we don't get a sense of wholeness from expressing opposites per se, but from letting go of the shame and guilt that have led to adopting the 'neurotic extremes' of aggression, self-effacement, or detached resignation. Integration of discarded aspects of the self will occur naturally as these conflicts are resolved.

Jung knew that embodying the wholeness of our personality was central to wellbeing, but his emphasis wasn't on looking at the past. Instead, his therapeutic approach was to correct the attitude of his patients towards opposite tendencies and encourage expression of both. Freud on the other hand focussed on the root of symptoms in the authority problems with our parents, and had little appreciation for Jung's notion of wholeness. Where Freud viewed neurotic symptoms as stemming from guilt and shame associated with past trauma, Jung saw aspects of a personality trying to emerge, albeit in conflict: *Where was the person trying to move?* And while Horney appreciated both our need to address conflicts of the past and to embody the wholeness of the personality, she (like Freud) didn't incorporate a transcendent Self in her theory.

The psycho-spiritual text *A Course in Miracles* provides a cohesive theory of healing that incorporates both the need to look at the root of shame and guilt and to experience wholeness. It places both of these needs within the context of a myth that emphasises our reality as an eternal, innocent, safe, whole (and wholly *loving*) Self, and is introduced in the next chapter.

Part Three

HEALING

7

A Course in Miracles

We all need a myth to live by — a philosophy of life that guides our decisions, defines our purpose and suggests how we can actualise it. Myths are stories that provide a framework for interpreting our past and present, and for imagining our future possibilities. While we mightn't think we subscribe to any particular myth or philosophy of life, we grow up immersed in the myths — represented by the defining values — of our immediate family and wider culture, and we will be influenced by them. Life comes at us from all directions and so we are always on the lookout for clues as to how to navigate it.

Religious myths provide answers to the 'Big Three' existential anxieties — loneliness, meaninglessness and death. The Christian creation myth and emphasis on the Fall addresses the anxiety of meaninglessness by suggesting that the purpose of life is to atone through suffering and sacrifice; the anxiety of death is addressed by a focus on the immortality of the soul and the possibility of happiness in an afterlife, and the anxiety of loneliness is abated by membership in a community as long as you obey the rules. These beliefs, though perhaps not prominent in today's increasingly secular society, were part of the fabric of medieval European society.

In contrast, the dominant secular myth in modern Western society (but still 'religious' in the sense of providing a meaning for existence) revolves around the notion of the heroic individual – the 'self-made man'. This myth tells us that the purpose of life is for the individual to strive for greatness through worldly achievement, overcoming adversity and obstacles, emerging a 'winner'. The anxiety of loneliness is abated by the promise that people will want to associate with us if we have something (power, status, money) that can 'rub off' on them or assist them in some way. To mitigate the fear of death, an emphasis on an immortal soul is replaced with what Ernest Becker in his book *The Denial of Death* called 'immortality projects': we can ensure that we live on in the world (rather than in an afterlife) through things we identify with or that carry our name, such as a building, children, an award, a street name, or even notoriety. This myth promises immortality through being remembered — that a trace of us will remain in the world as long as we do something significant enough to be noticed.

Though they are poles apart in their approaches to life's purpose — representing a 'guilt-prone' and 'shame-prone' approach respectively — both of these myths share in the idea that life is about escaping from a present state of unworthiness. In both cases there is a need to prove ourselves — either through suffering, sacrifice and self-negation, or through competitiveness, domination and self-inflation. *A Course in Miracles* provides an alternative myth that establishes that nothing we 'do or think or wish or make' is necessary to establish our worth, and that true happiness and security comes from this realisation.

Dreaming of Exile: Reimagining the Fall

> *The goal of the curriculum... is 'Know thyself.' There is nothing else to seek. Everyone is looking for himself and for the power and glory he thinks he has lost.*[81]
>
> A Course in Miracles

The philosophy of *A Course in Miracles* shares common elements with the higher philosophical teachings of Hinduism found in the Vedanta texts, composed around 800 BC. Central to these teachings is the idea that our unhappiness stems from a limited awareness that roots our identity in the world and the body — a world of conflict, decay, sickness and death. Consequently, we feel vulnerable and at odds with everyone and everything. The way out of our unhappiness, according to the Vedanta, is to expand our consciousness and awaken to our spiritual or 'true' Self that transcends the world and is invulnerable to the passage of time.

The Vedanta places the Self within the oneness of God and regards the material world as Maya, a great disguise in which the truth of the wholeness and magnitude of our Self is easily lost. The self that experiences itself as separate from God/Oneness is called the false or 'ego' self and when we identify with it, we feel vulnerable and incomplete — we have fallen asleep to who we really are, to the grandeur of our Self, and to a sense of peace that (to borrow from Saint Paul) surpasses all understanding.

Like the Vedanta, *A Course in Miracles* emphasises our reality as an integral part of God's Oneness. The Course's creation myth, however, is decidedly Gnostic in flavour and speaks to our feelings of shame and guilt. The Gnostics were a Christian group that emerged in the Mediterranean during the first century who developed their own creation myth to explain our experience in the world, particularly our sense of alienation — of never quite feeling at home no matter how much posterity we enjoy. There are many variations of the Gnostic myth but the most congruent with the Course's comes from the Gnostic philosopher Valentinus. In this myth, the world itself is the result of a cosmic fall.

The story begins with an original state of formless Oneness — an abstract unity between God and His emanations — that seems to be destroyed when an emanation called Sophia desires to create like her father instead of just being a creation. The desire itself is enough to spark a whole series of events leading to the making of the world; a place of decay and suffering. Mortified at the world she made, Sophia would have forgotten her true Home but that God took pity on her and placed Truth within her mind to console her — Truth being the memory of her origins and her true eternal state (her *Self*). Hence, the way out of suffering according to the Gnostics is to tap into Truth and remember our spiritual essence.

In the Course's myth there is the same wish arising in an aspect of Oneness to be *the* authority, but there is also the desire to stand apart from Oneness and be recognised as something special.[82] These desires were enough for the world to seem to arise — the unity of Oneness now replaced by a world of differentiation, chaos, change, competition and decay, in which we feel separate from our Source and each other. We see a world of opposites, of competing aims and needs, of love and hate and believe that God too is capable of both love and vengeance. No longer identified with Oneness, we literally feel a fragment of our former selves — an incomplete, vulnerable and *needy* self, fearful of the God whose Oneness we think we have destroyed and mournful for the Love we believe we have rejected (but through the process of projection, now believe has rejected and abandoned *us*).

The 'good news' is that because a part of Oneness can't really think apart from the rest, we have never separated from God. He is as close to us as He ever was, and our wholeness remains intact. However, with our attention rooted in the world with its attendant struggles, we fall asleep to the memory of Truth within our minds. Feeling separate from perfect Love we assume that a fall has occurred; hence our feelings of incompleteness, vulnerability, shame, guilt, depression and anxiety.

Whether we consciously believe in the God of the Abrahamic religions — an arbiter of justice and agent of punishment and reward — we've all at some stage had the experience of feeling overlooked and punished by something larger than ourselves, whether that be a parent, government, country, or sporting team. *A Course in Miracles* addresses these feelings, proposing that an unconscious 'authority problem' between ourselves and God (reflected in our relationships with our parents and other significant authority figures) is at the root of our distress, including the anxieties of loneliness, meaninglessness and death. We are 'at home in God, dreaming of exile' (T-10.I.2:1).

The Path to Remembrance

One of the main ways the Gnostics sought to connect with Truth was to avoid involvement with the world and the body. Either they chose a path of asceticism in which they tried to ignore their bodily needs and desires, or they chose to do the exact opposite and flout conventional morality in an attempt to demonstrate their freedom from the world. These 'libertines' lived a life of excess and (according to accounts from Church authorities who were hostile toward the Gnostics) extraordinary depravity.[83] The Valentinians however chose a middle path in which they looked after the health of their bodies and followed the Ten Commandments and the Sermon on the Mount as ethical guides. They focussed on living a good and just life, devotion to good works, and dispensing alms to the poor.[84]

The focus on loving service as a means of remembering the love and unity of God's Oneness is also found in the Vedanta and *A Course in Miracles* which emphasise that the way we connect with the truth of our unity with God (and each other) is through unselfishness and love. The approach of these philosophies isn't to spend copious amounts of time contemplating the nature of the divine or trying to have an experience of Oneness or 'no-self' as is the case in some Eastern traditions. *A Course in Miracles* makes it clear that seeking communion in a direct fashion is a long and arduous path. Likewise, in *The Bhagavad Gita* (a Hindu text of the Vedanta philosophy) Prince Arjuna asks Lord Krishna whether holy work — work infused with a higher purpose — or renunciation of the world is the best path. Krishna replies that it is difficult to have an awareness of divinity through renouncing the world or through contemplation alone. Better the 'Yoga of holy work' — work conducted without 'selfish bonds' but with love.

There is, however, a significant difference between the Course's concept of loving service and those of the Vedanta and the Valentinian Gnostics. The latter talk of *cultivating* loving kindness and compassion, and of being unselfish in our works. In contrast, the Course focuses on *removing the obstacles* to love (shame and guilt), rather than on love's cultivation. In the Course's system, it's shame, guilt and the fear they generate that make us self-centred and judgemental. Undoing shame and guilt allows us to automatically be peaceful and genuinely compassionate and kind: 'Your task is not to seek for love, but merely to seek and find all the barriers within yourself that you have built against it' (T-16.IV.6).

It is our inner experience of exile — of being far from the comfort of our Source — that is the ultimate origin of our shame and guilt, but we're not asked to address our relationship to God directly. By undoing shame and guilt regarding specific relationships, we slowly grow into an experience that affirms the message of the Course's mythology — that we remain whole and in perfect safety and love — and so we become more loving. The Course calls the process of undoing shame and guilt 'forgiveness', however it's definition of forgiveness is unique.

The Problem of Forgiveness

The concept of forgiveness is currently enjoying popularity in psychology. Indeed, you'd be hard-pressed to find a therapist who hasn't observed a link between holding grievances and stress. However, our ideas of what forgiveness is and how it comes about can be deeply problematic. In an *ABC News* investigation into the relationship between religion and domestic violence, problems with the traditional Christian concept of forgiveness are clear. Reviewing two hundred interviews with domestic violence survivors, social workers, clergy, church staff and theologians, researchers found many women had been told to simply 'forgive' and return to abusive husbands, which led to enduring further violent behaviour.[85]

This view of forgiveness looks at the behaviour and says, no we don't condone it, it is terrible, even 'evil', and yes you have endured much harm because of it. Subsequently, it is suggested that a victim should simply rise above the pain and hurt and no longer hold a grudge, which sounds just as reasonable as asking them to pull a rabbit out of a hat. Yet it is this 'magic trick' that commonly goes by the name of forgiveness.

This is why Freud referred to the New Testament credo 'love thine enemies' as '*credo quia absurdum*' or 'I believe it because it is absurd'.[86] To Freud, it is impossible to love someone — or forgive them — if we feel they have diminished us in some way, and so striving to fulfil the love-command can only lead to more shame and guilt. Pretending otherwise is an exercise in denial, leaving the door wide open for our fears and anger to be expressed in more destructive (and often seemingly unrelated) ways.

The essential point is that we can't move beyond blame and hatred if we feel damaged by someone. Likewise, the only way we can rise above unkind treatment at the hands of others is when we no longer feel it has damaged us, and ultimately this depends on who and what we think we are.

Forgiveness Redefined

> *Belief that there is another way of perceiving is the loftiest idea of which ego thinking is capable. That is because it contains a hint of recognition that the ego is not the Self.*[87]
>
> A Course in Miracles

The Course's definition of forgiveness revolves around the premise that we are never upset by a fact but by our interpretation of it. This is reminiscent of a major tenet of Stoic philosophy and many others, including Albert Ellis's Rational Emotive

Behaviour Therapy, the forerunner to Cognitive Behavioural Therapy: it's not circumstances but our interpretation of them that disturbs or excites us. If someone belittles us, for example, the anger or fear we feel is because they have triggered feelings of inferiority or guilt.

An example from the life of Socrates helps to illustrate this idea. Socrates was often ridiculed for his unorthodox discussions, but this didn't seem to faze him. In an episode from his book *Lives and Opinions of Eminent Philosophers,* the third century Greek biographer Diogenes Laertius paints a scene in which Socrates is mocked, shoved around and beaten when passionately engaged in trying to get his point across; yet the great philosopher bears it 'patiently', so much so that someone questions why. Socrates replied, 'If an ass had kicked me, would I bring an action against him?'[88] Socrates perceived the actions of his attackers as stemming from ignorance — if they knew better, they'd do better. But it was the absence of shame or guilt in Socrates' that enabled him to not take the actions of his attackers personally.

Shame and guilt root our identification in our separated ego-self and cut us off from the integrity, wholeness and invulnerability of our Self. The more shame and guilt we let go of, the greater our connection with the security of our Self and our inherent worthiness. This is why Socrates didn't fear life or his impending death when sentenced to drink hemlock, but seemed happy regardless of his circumstances — he knew that the essential part of himself couldn't be touched. Importantly (and related to the later discussion of 'form versus content' in Chapter Eight), though Socrates didn't defend himself verbally or physically when he was being mocked and shoved about, he could just as likely have restrained his attackers or rebuked them if that is what his Self moved him to do, but — in touch with his own worth — he wouldn't be coming from a defensive *attitude* or hatred.

The fact that our Self can't be harmed is why Socrates disagreed with his friend Polus who suggested it is worse to be on the receiving end of a wrong than to be the perpetrator, because of the suffering involved. Socrates replied that it is infinitely worse to be the agent of evil than the recipient because to do wrong closes the door on our soul, and this can only lead to feelings of despair. Indeed, if the receiver of harm knows who they really are, they might experience pain or suffer physical harm, but on another level it won't disturb them because they're identified with the integrity of their soul. The only real harm we can do to anyone is to *ourselves* when we misplace our identification. As the Stoic philosopher Marcus Aurelius wrote:

> *Begin the morning by saying to thyself, I shall meet with the busybody, the ungrateful, arrogant, deceitful, envious, unsocial. All these things happen to them by reason of their ignorance of what is good and evil. But... I can neither be injured by any of them, for no one can fix on me what is ugly...*[89]

That last line from Aurelius — 'for no one can fix on me what is ugly' — is really the heart of forgiveness. A shift in identification from a shameful and guilty self to one of wholeness and holiness is the Course's definition of healing and the process whereby we forgive. In other words, you could say forgiveness is the healing of our self-concept.

Recalling Jung's theory on archetypes, we're not born a blank slate: we are inclined to perceive things in a certain way. And this way, according to the Course, arises from a self-concept predicated on shame and guilt for our (imagined) separation from God, reinforced in our lives first and foremost through interactions with our parents and other authority figures. Every situation therefore is viewed through the lens of shame and guilt and interpreted accordingly, but it's not the situations per se that are the primary cause of our distress.

Forgiveness therefore isn't achieved by trying to overlook what someone has done, but by addressing our feelings of shame and guilt associated with it. Forgiveness is really about undoing beliefs about ourselves that seem tied to an event or person. It's a process whereby we look at what we think another's behaviour says about how they regard us, and then refuse to agree with them — this is what leads to our freedom from the past and allows forgiveness to simply *be*.

Importantly, the first step in the process of forgiveness is to acknowledge the hurt, pain and anger associated with being mistreated. However, forgiveness's end is the ultimate statement of release: that our inner peace and sense of wholeness can't be held to ransom by the vicissitudes of circumstance.

Another major distinction between the Course's forgiveness and the traditional concept is that forgiveness as the Course defines it is a process that occurs in the mind: it doesn't necessarily mean that we physically reconcile with someone, or that we don't seek legal redress, or that we stay in a broken relationship. Forgiveness doesn't relate to any particular behaviour but only to our *attitude*. It is possible, for example, that through the process of forgiveness we decide it is best for all concerned that contact is terminated — but this needn't be done from a punitive attitude.

Unfortunately, what generally passes for forgiveness fails to make this distinction between attitude and behaviour and is anything but a healing process. For a guilt-prone person in a relationship with someone who's adopted an extreme form of the aggressive solution, for example, it might be near impossible to achieve any compromise in which their own needs are considered: there's no middle ground for extreme aggressive types — it's their way, *all the way*, or nothing at all. In such cases, the guilt-prone person's forgiveness process might call for them to leave, perhaps reflecting a realisation that they're not responsible for their partner's happiness (or lack thereof), that they're capable of surviving outside of the relationship, and that they have a right to be happy.

As we heal our identification with shame and guilt, we will no longer experience hatred or fear toward the person we thought had diminished us, or perhaps we'll no longer think of them at all. This is an important point for survivors of severe interpersonal trauma such as physical, emotional or sexual abuse, particularly in the early stages of therapy. For many people, forgiveness happens over time but is not the focus of therapy: processing the trauma, reassessing beliefs about the self and learning to function well again in the world are the means for moving on. In this regard, we can say forgiveness is a state in which we are no longer at the mercy of intruding thoughts about the event or the person, nor do we blame them for how we are feeling now.

Miracles Redefined

The 'miracle' that the Course's title is based on doesn't relate to a shift in external circumstances (as the Bible uses the term), but rather to the change in perspective that sees ourselves as whole regardless of our past. This shift occurs after we've addressed the shame and guilt associated with particular events and circumstances. The miracle is when we are no longer haunted by the past or fearful of the future, but feel peace in the present instead.

While the idea that it's our interpretations of things that upset us rather than the things themselves is central to forgiveness, we can fall into denial if we believe we *shouldn't* become disturbed by what happens around us. The aim isn't to be unmoved by anything. Rather, the invitation is to avoid *justifying* an ongoing attachment to our judgements and anger. This is usually something we can only bring ourselves to consider after some time: the road to this ideal requires work and is a process.

The neurologist and psychotherapist Victor Frankl had a formula for despair: despair equals suffering without meaning.[90] I'd qualify this by saying despair equals suffering without *positive* meaning. All of us are meaning-makers — you could say it's what distinguishes the human species from all others. It's why humans are storytellers; we are giving meaning to things *all the time*. When we are identified with shame and guilt, the unconscious stories we tell ourselves serve to strengthen that identification. We take things personally, regarding difficult situations as being hostile towards us (*Why does this always happen to me? It's not fair!*). A way out of our despair, therefore, is to regard each trial as an opportunity to become aware of our identification with shame and guilt so we can move beyond it.

Help: The Bridge Between Worlds

Where *A Course in Miracles* departs most significantly from what can be viewed as a purely psychological approach, is in its emphasis on seeking help from beyond the world. Because the help asked for is of a transcendent order, I will capitalise it to distinguish it from 'worldly' help, such as therapy or emotional support from loved ones.

The Help that we invite in to our lives is the memory of Truth, which speaks of the reality of our Self. The Course uses the term 'Holy Spirit' to symbolise that aspect of our mind that is aware of both the flawed being we think we are and the glorious reality of our Self. It can therefore provide solace and guidance in every difficulty we face: the Holy Spirit is our 'Guide through a far country', a communication link to our Self (C-6.4:6).

We can use any symbol of non-judgemental wisdom and love as a tangible way of relating to Truth or the Holy Spirit. Calling on Help from people who symbolise ego-transcendence, such as the Buddha or Socrates (who himself had his 'Daimon'), can be of great benefit. For Carl Jung, Philemon — a wise, kind and spiritual person who appeared in Ovid's *Metamorphoses,* in Goethe's *Faust,* and in a dream of Jung's during his period of inner crisis — was such a symbol. Jung painted a portrait of Philemon and placed it on the wall above his bed at his holiday residence, and this connection was of great help to him.

It isn't essential to call on a religious figure for Help — any symbol of a loving, egoless, wise and non-judgmental presence will do. To borrow a phrase from Alcoholics Anonymous, it doesn't matter what your symbol is, *as long as it isn't you*. Since we are so identified with our ego, we need a symbol that we can easily relate to as something outside of it, beyond its influence.

Asking for Help is important because left to our own devices we're likely to experience shame and guilt as insurmountable. We are so rooted to our past, the lessons of the world and the self-concept we have identified with, that it is very difficult for us to see beyond them. When we are identified with shame and guilt, our default position is to interpret things in a way that confirms our existing beliefs and fears — what psychologists call the 'confirmation bias' — and we'll be sure we are right.

Essentially, asking for Help requires a receptive attitude which, in turn, opens the door to a transcendent source of guidance and consolation that reminds us of who we are and of our eternal safety. Asking for Help can also make us feel accompanied on our journey. After all, implicit in the belief in separation is the idea that — despite everything around us — we are essentially alone. And since all of our distress can be traced back to the thought that we usurped God's role as the authority, asking for Help is also the way out of guilt — it means we're not trying to possess the place of knowledge whilst our inner two-year-old cries, '*Me* do it!'. This in turn mitigates fear.

We don't have to believe in the reality of something beyond our self to benefit from its influence, but be willing to suspend any *dis*belief so that our experience can gradually teach us. This is the 'leap of faith' required to set our path towards a better inner experience. We can debate metaphysical realities and the true nature of existence, but the value of such debate is, well, debatable. The Buddha refused to answer metaphysical questions. He explained himself with the following metaphor: if you are in a burning house, you don't stop to carry out a detailed analysis of how the fire started. *You get out of the house!*

Likewise, in order to have a more peaceful experience in the world we don't need to forensically examine spiritual questions that are beyond anyone's rational comprehension. The way out of our suffering is to diligently adhere to certain practices; this leads to an experience that satisfies our need for answers because in the experience there are simply no questions. It is important to ensure that a preoccupation with metaphysical speculation doesn't become a way of avoiding this experience.

Guidance and Synchronicity

The road to accepting and expressing our wholeness is difficult, painful and perilous, however it will rise to meet us when we embark on it, and we'll be guided and supported along the way. There are many ways our receptivity to Help can be answered.

Being authentic means going with your truth even though you fear the loss of security. We all want to have the strength and resolve to step beyond our insecurities and be true to what feels right to us. We want to be true to ourselves and know we will be safe. The message of Jung, Socrates and many of the great mystics is that nothing is worth turning your back on your inner guidance for, and the greatest freedom lies in knowing that as long as you're true to *that,* you'll always have enough to get by, even though at times this can seem like barely enough.

The concept of divine providence plays a central role in many religions and is relevant to our discussion of guidance and security. In theology, providence refers to God's foresight and ability to see the whole picture, and to intervene in the world accordingly. In relation to the Course, God doesn't intervene in the world. The concept of providence, however, suggests we will get what we need when forgiveness and the integrity of our Self — our 'holiness' as Christians might put it, or our 'wholeness' as Jung would put it — is our goal. For many, providence relates to 'going with the flow'. It's about being in tune with the Self, or whatever name works for us as a symbol of our highest nature, and working *with* it. Mother Teresa, for example, wrote of her faith in Jesus: 'If He wants something done, He gives us the means. If He doesn't provide us with the means, then He doesn't want that work done'.[91] This captures beautifully how a belief in providence — as guidance, not as reward or punishment —

assists our goal of wholeness.

A Jungian parallel with providence would be synchronicity. Synchronicity was a term Jung coined to describe meaningful coincidences. A coincidence is when two or more things occur at the same time, seem related, but have no causal connection. If you suddenly think of a friend you haven't heard from for years and then they call you, that is a coincidence — there is no linear cause–effect relationship between thinking of your friend and receiving the phone call. Synchronicity describes coincidences in which an inner psychological process is met with an external event that appears to directly 'answer' or reflect that process. We can, for example, happen upon a sentence in a book or a television program (or overhear a conversation) that seems to speak directly to our need at the time. *How* meaningful coincidences occur was not the concern of Jung. *That* they occur is an empirical fact.

The essential element of synchronicity is that is serves as a guide. This type of thinking is generally foreign to the modern Western mind, however the ancient Chinese (and medieval Europeans) were concerned with the chance nature of events and how, taken together, they form a guide for our psychological and spiritual growth. For example, in my work as a therapist I would sometimes receive a cluster of clients with similar issues which reflected my own psychological 'zeitgeist', and this gave me a heads-up regarding thoughts and attitudes that had been simmering away in the background of my consciousness, things I needed to pay more attention to.

Generally speaking, the Western mind is concerned with manipulating and acting upon nature to make it serve our own needs and desires. We are used to imposing ourselves on it, having dominion over it. The traditional Eastern mindset is very different. It focuses on situating ourselves in respect to the whole and respecting the interconnectedness of all things. It is therefore about listening, tuning in and being receptive. In this respect, the concept of providence is in line with the East's emphasis on receptivity, as illustrated in the following quote from one of the sisters working with Mother Teresa: 'We need to be flexible — when it's God's time things are easy and when it's not His time things are difficult. We must really listen to the invitation that God extends to us in whichever way it is manifested'.[92]

Central to the idea of providence is that of leading a Eucharistic life — one of communion and receptivity. Likewise, Jung talks of the importance of being receptive to the will of what he sometimes calls the collective unconscious and sometimes God: we need to admit that there are some problems we can't solve on our own, and by doing this we 'prepare the ground' to receive helpful ideas or thoughts.[93]

Jung appreciated that the goal of holiness and the goal of wholeness of the personality are related. He equated God's will with the will of our unconscious, by which he meant the way in which we need to move in order to express the wholeness of our personality and Self. His repeated advice to people facing an important decision was that they must listen to their unconscious. Was it fully aligned with their conscious decision? This would help them see if they were 'at one' with themselves about it.[94] For Jung, looking at dreams was one such way of listening, and heeding the messages of synchronicity was another.

Jung cautioned that our ability to cope with what's before us in the second half of life depends more vitally on the presence of a deep inner movement towards it: if what we embark upon doesn't stem from an inner imperative (but from ideas about what we 'should' do for example) we'll experience it as an insurmountable struggle, and come out less secure and confident than we did going in. On the other hand, anything that we do that's in accordance with our Self falls within our emotional capacity and resilience, regardless of its objectively challenging nature.

A wonderful illustration of this can be found in the story of Corrie Ten Boom, a Dutch woman who, along with her family, helped hide and relocate Jews in the second World War during the Nazi occupation of Holland. Up until her work with the Resistance, Corrie's sole occupation was as a watchmaker in her father's business in the family home, which was a secure and happy environment. When Corrie was fifty-two, Germany invaded Holland and her world became anything but safe. Feeling that work in the Resistance was in line with her inner guidance, she found the strength and fortitude to carry out her part with amazing courage and capability. Eventually, her and her family's activities were discovered by the Nazis, and all of them were sent to concentration camps in Germany.

When Corrie was released from her ordeal (over a year later) and returned to Holland she was approached to resume her work with the Resistance. She obliged and her first mission was to hand-deliver false release papers for a prisoner in jail to a (German-controlled) police station. When she entered the station and the doors closed behind her, she was consumed with anxiety. Her hands were shaking as she handed over the documents to an officer she nearly exposed as a member of the Resistance by greeting him by name, and before he had finished asking her to return the following day she was on her way out. Corrie concluded that whatever bravery she had shown previously working for the Resistance was a loan from God 'of the talent needed to do a job', and since she no longer had the skills to do it, it was no longer what she was being called to do.[95]

Corrie now knew that the 'something else' she was looking for upon her return home didn't lie in working with the Resistance. Shortly after this experience at the police station she remembered her sister Betsy's dream of the two of them establishing a place of rehabilitation for people after the war. Betsy had died along with Corrie's father in the camps, however Corrie decided that if establishing such a place was in accordance with a greater will, then the means would be provided for it to be done. And indeed, they were, through what only can be described as moments of synchronicity or — more in line with Corrie's theology — providence, and her new occupation was a profound source of inspiration and happiness for her.

Whenever we ask for Help (either consciously or not), there will be a reaction to our request in a form that is meaningful to us. I had such an experience during a major point in writing this book. After years of insisting that I wouldn't include any material about *A Course in Miracles,* I went through a major period of inner turmoil around closing my professional practice and ending my career as a Rolfer. Though I hadn't associated my self-imposed embargo on discussing the Course with this turmoil (and I never made any conscious attempt to address it), I nonetheless found that as time passed it simply fell away. One day shortly after deciding that I would write about the Course, I noticed a folded piece of A4 paper lying on the floor in the centre of my study. I left the paper where it was and walked around it throughout the day as I went to and from my desk. Finally, when I stood to leave the room, I looked at the paper and decided to pick it up. Unfolding it I read:

Dear Steph,

Congratulations! You get an A.

The message struck a chord. Many years earlier I had written a letter to Kenneth Wapnick (a Course teacher) regarding the Course's theory. The letter I picked up from the floor was Ken's (always succinct!) reply, which must have dropped onto the floor when I moved some folders earlier in the day. (Sorry for not taking better care of your letters, Ken!) But my lack of due diligence worked in my favour that day. I felt I had been given the nod regarding the book's new direction, from someone who's opinion I respected.

Not all 'signposts' affirm the path we're taking. Some moments of synchronicity shout 'Wrong way. Go back'. Patty Schemel experienced a striking example of this after she left her band and was living on the streets. One day she walked past a church and through the open doors saw a drum kit. It reminded her that she played the drums — since being homeless she had forgotten about her earlier life and that she had a skill and talent. 'You don't have to keep doing this', was the message of the kit, and eventually, playing the drums provided a means of return for Schemel.

Moreover, being receptive doesn't mean we should *look* for coincidences — that would be using our conscious, rational mind to try and make connections that may or may not be there. Synchronicity is more mysterious and peculiar than that. Connections hit us, seemingly out of the blue, with their meaning.

It's more of an arresting experience, an 'a-ha' that stops us in our tracks, not unlike the moment a work of art strikes us with its beauty. Which brings me to another form of help we receive along the road — reminders of Who we are.

Remembrance and Beauty

Emotional and physical pain anchors our awareness to our physical and psychological bodies — to the limited awareness of 'I' with all the sorrow and anxiety, desire and loathing associated with it. It's little wonder that during stressful times we can feel a need to shake ourselves off — to get away from ourselves (hence the attraction of drugs and alcohol). However there are things that help to transport us in a way that is helpful, and they do this because they remind us of the beauty of our Self.

Many people find the arts enrich them in ways they can't explain, but their transportive function is sure to be an underlying attraction. As the Irish novelist James Joyce wrote, when we are struck by the beauty of a work of art, 'The mind is arrested and raised above desire and loathing'.[96] In other words, we're raised above our self that craves some things and is repelled by others. The best art, according to Joyce — 'proper' art — inspires in us 'aesthetic arrest'. We are so moved by a connection that we are stopped in our tracks. Likewise, the American philosopher Ralph Waldo Emerson appreciated the ability of the arts, and music in particular, to provide us with a refuge from our fevered self: 'So is music an asylum. It takes us out of the actual and whispers to us dim secrets that startle our wonder as to who we are, and for what, whence, and whereto'.[97]

Where synchronicity strikes us with meaning at an intellectual level (we see a link between inner and outer events) and serves as a guide, a connection with beauty hits us at an emotional level and speaks to our longing. All forms of art can be a potent means of speaking to our deepest yearnings; they comfort us in ways the intellect can't. The power of music to do this was discussed in Oliver Sacks' book *Musicophilia*. Sacks described how many people found that music and nothing else had the power to relieve them of depression. Sacks himself had this experience after his mother's death: it was the random exposure to a piece of music by Schubert (emanating from a basement window as he walked by) that had him smiling and feeling alive in what had been weeks of emotional numbness. Music wasn't a magic pill — Sacks' depression returned — but it did offer respite and a reminder of what was still within reach.

Though some works of art can help lift us out of ourselves, our ability to experience the transporting effects of beauty isn't limited to them. As Socrates said: 'the one thing that makes that object beautiful is the presence in it or the association with it, in whatever way the relation comes about, of absolute beauty'.[98] Those moments in which we connect with the beauty of a piece of music and it transforms how we feel, we are connecting with Absolute Beauty, or what Socrates otherwise called the Good, and Truth.

Absolute Beauty (synonymous with the beauty of our Self) is the transporting agent, not the work of art itself, which is the vessel. This is why we can have an experience of Beauty in a variety of circumstances. The eighteenth-century poet William Cowper for example was plagued by recurring bouts of major depression and experienced the 'inefficacy of all human means' to alleviate them, yet had a brief reprieve one day as he contacted beauty in nature: 'The morning was clear and calm; the sun shone bright upon the sea. Here it was that all of a sudden, as if another sun had been kindled that instant in the heavens on purpose to dispel sorrow and vexation of spirit, I felt the weight of all my misery taken off; my heart became light and joyful in a moment'.[99]

Anything then, can be a vehicle for an experience of Absolute Beauty when we need it — even a smile or a kind gesture from someone can strike us in a profound way, offering a momentary feeling of liberation as we have a sense of being transported beyond ourselves and the pains and anxieties associated with our bodily identification.

This being said, it is likely that there will be specific things that work best for us in connecting to the beauty of our Self, and we'll receive guidance as to what these might be. During the period following the closure of my professional practice, I had a dream in which I held an envelope that I knew had been given to me as a gift. Opening it I found two tickets to a Chopin concert. As a teenager, listening to a cassette of *The Best of Chopin* helped me go to sleep, and although I still had an appreciation for classical music as an adult, I'd forgotten how helpful it had been for me in the past. The fact that I received two tickets meant that I wouldn't be alone when I listened to the music. As Beethoven said of composing, 'I'm never alone when I'm alone'. Likewise, for Patty Schemel, seeing the drum kit in the church wasn't only helpful in pointing her towards a tangible way out of her financial predicament, but reminded her of what had given her peace before.

Unfortunately, though we can find something that helps to take us out of ourselves, it's unlikely that it will have a profound effect on us all the time. Sacks was met with this realisation a few days after hearing Schubert's music through the basement window. He went to see a performance of Schubert's *Winterreise* hoping to once again feel alive, but was unmoved. He couldn't demand the music to work its wonders, its power 'must steal on one unawares, come spontaneously as a blessing or a grace'.[100]

The reason something can move us in a profound way one day and not the next relates to our resistance to letting go of our bodily identification (something that is explored in more depth in the following chapter). It might seem masochistic to say we would prefer our pain to an experience of peace, but to join with our Self means to be transported beyond our identification with the ego self that clings to 'I', 'me', and 'mine', and it is *this* we are afraid of. As the following passage from the Course explains, when we have an experience of being transported beyond ourselves, we have *lost our fear of union* with our Self (which is a part of a non-differentiated unity), and have experienced a sudden expansion of awareness that embraces it:

> *What really happens is that you have... lost your fear of union... And while this lasts you are not uncertain of your Identity, and would not limit It. You have escaped from fear to peace... (T-18.VI.11:7, 9-10).*

In these instants of release from our pain there is no thought about the past, future, or present. Fear is replaced by an experience of peace and joy — something that in our usual state of awareness can seem beyond the realms of possibility considering our external circumstances. When our fear of union lessens, that 'special something' (music, art, nature, a memory) can gently take us to the horizon where our self and Self meet.

8

The How of Forgiveness

Guilt demands we deny ourselves the pleasures of the world in order to atone; shame demands we prove our worth by accumulating power or recognition. Though our solutions are designed to keep us safe they come with a profound sense of loss:

> *Many have chosen to renounce the world while still believing its reality. And they have suffered from a sense of loss, and have not been released accordingly. Others have chosen nothing but the world, and they have suffered from a sense of loss still deeper, which they did not understand (W-155.4:2-4).*

Between the self-effacing and aggressive solutions lies a middle path born of a sense of wholeness that helps us fully engage with life. Forgiveness is a means of experiencing this.

Withdrawing Our Projections

The first step in forgiveness is acknowledging that we're never upset by a fact but by our interpretation of it. This is important and empowering because it focusses our attention on the mind rather than emphasising what is going on externally. This in itself can help to diffuse the intensity of our reaction by providing a degree of detachment — we are able to step into an 'observer' role once we have taken back our power from the situation.

The next step addresses the way we feel about ourselves and others. Instead of thinking that we feel awful because someone else treated us a certain way, we open our minds to two possibilities: firstly, that the real cause of our distress is that we secretly believe that we deserve to be treated unkindly or unfairly (otherwise we wouldn't have taken things personally); secondly, that what we judge harshly in someone else is something we ourselves do or have done in the past though it might have looked differently.

If for example we are outraged at someone's selfishness, we can be sure that we have also accused ourselves of being selfish and have condemned ourselves for it. 'Would I condemn myself for doing this?' is a question the Course suggests we ask whenever we feel angered by what someone else does (W-134.15:3). This gives us an opportunity to release both the other person and ourselves from condemnation. The intensity of our reaction can also indicate that we have neglected to develop the positive correlate of what we have judged against: if selfishness in others disgusts us, it is likely that we don't engage in enough *self-nurture*, or listening to what it is we really want to do or not do. Likewise, the person who struggles to stop working and be still for a while can angrily label others as lazy; however, deep down they may yearn for the ability to rest without anxiety.

Once we are willing to entertain the idea that we're upset because we're perceiving outside of us what we have condemned in ourselves, we are ready for the last step: asking for Help to look on both ourselves and the other person differently. By asking for Help we become available to the memory of our invulnerable and complete Self and our feelings of neediness and victimisation will lessen. This frees us from our insistence that another person's behaviour needs to change in order for us to feel better: we take back responsibility for our emotional state in recognition that the problem lies with our own self-concept. And then, to paraphrase the Course, we might feel better because loving then seems possible to us (T-10.I.3:3). Initially, we might still feel out of sorts, but little by little, as we keep seeing the problem as it is (our identification with shame and guilt), not the way we've set it up (someone else's behaviour) we'll begin to feel less anxious and defensive. This doesn't mean that we never address behavioural issues in someone else, but that if we do it comes from a place of kindness rather than attack.

When someone's behaviour has us worrying about ourselves — Did we say something wrong? Are we annoying them? Do they love us? Do they respect us? — we can be sure that we have identified with shame and guilt. All uncertainty, says the Course, is really doubt about ourselves, which leads us to react defensively. It can feel awful not knowing where we stand with someone — if we identify with our ego, we don't have the external validation we need to protect us from shame and guilt, and so we get anxious and angry. The fundamental cause of our distress is this identification with the ego and the sense of vulnerability and inadequacy at its core.

Earliest Memories and Our Style of Life

If we look back at our lives, we'll see that our solution has a long history. Events will stand out as being congruent with the general themes of feeling abandoned (not good enough) and punished (bad). Indeed, the psychoanalyst Alfred Adler proposed that our 'style of life' is revealed in the first things we can remember from childhood.

Whether the memories are accurate or not, the fact that we have selected these particular memories suggests that they represent the major themes contributing to our overall style of life. For example, one of Adler's clients recalled that her family had a family portrait taken when she was four years old. Her brother was given a ball to hold and was placed on the arm of the chair, while she was told to stand on the other side and wasn't given anything.[101] This early memory, easily recalled, formed part of a series of memories with similar themes centring on the idea of not being good enough, and the client's style of life was driven by these themes — the events that stood out for her were those which confirmed a belief in her inferiority and rejection.

That we live our life by stories and that these stories shape our thoughts, decisions and behaviour is the main principle of Narrative Therapy. People construct and are constructed by their survival stories from childhood which are reinforced throughout their lives. It's true that we can encounter many similar circumstances in life, however memory is selective and our narratives are biased towards highlighting experiences that fit with the script. Our narratives are the backdrop to our solutions and provide the primary frame of reference for our interpretations. We don't perceive everything that we see: only that which fits with our 'style of life'.[102]

When the message of the story (and our solution) is no longer helpful — that is, when we're no longer satisfied with identifying as a survivor of a painful past and with our solution — we can experience a crisis point. This was the case for Maria, a client who had adopted the compliant solution in an attempt to keep herself safe. Maria's earliest memory was of standing as a toddler and (literally) crying for attention from her father who responded with a smack so forceful it knocked her down and winded her. Other childhood experiences in which Maria put herself 'out there' and that ended badly formed the basis for her adoption of compliance and self-effacement as a way of life.

A Study in Forgiveness

Maria sought help shortly after returning from an overseas holiday with her husband, George. She'd been reluctant to go on the trip, but in the end — as was her pattern — she acquiesced. From the moment the holiday was booked, Maria silently lamented having to go.

Denying herself to please others wasn't something new for Maria; she'd spent a lifetime doing it. The difference in this scenario was that she had reached a point in her life where she'd well and truly had enough of self-sacrifice, but she wasn't yet conscious that she'd reached this point, and her inner conflict manifested in anxiety. Maria was highly agitated on the day of the flight and her anxiety peaked once she boarded the plane and took her seat. In a moment of clarity, Maria realised that she needed to put in a concentrated effort to calm down, otherwise she would find herself in the grips of a full blown panic attack. She silently asked for Help (Maria was a student of *A Course in Miracles*), and then the thought occurred to her to practice a mindfulness technique.

Maria observed the thoughts racing through her mind, most of them relating to the impending doom of a panic attack, of wanting to get off the plane, and of how she wished she had said no to George. She tried to observe her thoughts non-judgementally without holding on to their storyline, and kept bringing her mind back to her breath. After several minutes of determined practice, she felt a deep sense of peace and relief come over her, and when she opened her eyes, she heard the following unmistakable words: 'That's the power of forgiveness'. Then the realisation hit her. Ever since she had said yes to going on the holiday, she had been harbouring a deep resentment towards George — firstly for making it so difficult (in her mind) for her to say no, and secondly because she was doing what she didn't really want to do.

Maria's anxiety had been exacerbated by her repressed anger toward her husband. Her decision to try and calm herself down and her request for Help reflected a willingness to let go of feeling victimised by George, even though she didn't realise this at the time.

Discerning the Voice of our Higher Self

Maria's difficulty in saying and sticking by what she wanted reflected a lack of self-trust in making decisions based on what she wanted or felt was right. It seems Maria hadn't listened to her Self when she agreed to go on the holiday. Discerning when it is the voice of our Self or of shame and guilt can, however, be a tricky business and we need to ask for Help in the process of discernment. The call of our solutions is so seductive and our fear of going against them so great, that in asking for Help and getting a sense that it would be best to go along with something mightn't be a 'Helpful' message at all.

A good indicator that a guilt-prone person has fallen into this trap is when they find themselves rationalising their compliance — 'After all, it's nice to make people happy'. This also shows their emotional investment in pleasing people. For the compliant person, it's important to remember that suffering plays such a large role in their solution that an unconscious attraction to sabotaging their own happiness may also be at play. Likewise, a shame-prone person's idea that 'just one drink/gamble/confrontation' couldn't hurt, could be the call of their solution. The old adage, 'If in doubt, don't', might be helpful to remember in such circumstances.

Gaps in the Narrative

After the holiday, Maria found that many grievances associated with her past and her parents surfaced as she began looking at how she related to her husband. Not only was George's behaviour challenging in its own right, George had become the screen onto which Maria projected all her pent-up hostility towards past figures who'd made it difficult for her to express her needs. After asking for Help around her anger towards her parents, Maria found herself at times spontaneously recalling inconsistencies in her 'narrative' — times when she *did* receive care and affection.

These recollections were prompted by seemingly unrelated things Maria read in a magazine or while watching a movie — when we're ready to move on, anything can serve as an instrument for healing. Maria also gained insight into her parents' upbringing through coincidental things, such as happening upon a documentary about the Italian village they grew up in, which helped her gain a new perspective of their behaviour, feel some compassion for them, and not take their harsh treatment of her so personally.

In a way, Maria's husband can be seen as the devil's advocate; his insistence that they go on a holiday provided an opportunity for Maria to work through her guilt and anxiety and stand firm. While she wasn't able to do this before going on the holiday, after her in-flight experience she was able to put her insights into practice, watching her mind for her tendency to acquiesce and for the fear associated with saying no. She could see that each instance of repressing her needs was a choice to feel victimised and that she'd feel negatively toward her husband once this had occurred.

Another aspect to Maria's difficulty in expressing herself was her feelings of dependency on George. Despite the fact that she worked part-time, managed the household budget and the household as a whole (Maria and George had two teenage children), Maria had exaggerated fears of being unable to care for herself if George ever died or left her. Part of her distress when her desires clashed with George's came from a fear that if she upset him, he might leave and that she wouldn't be able to cope in the world by herself. In adopting a compliant solution, Maria's self-concept was rooted in a sense of powerlessness despite the fact that she was a very capable person.

Part of Maria's forgiveness process involved seeing the inconsistencies in her dependency narrative, recognising that she already did many things that showed she could survive in the world without a partner if it came to that, and that her fears of abandonment were more likely the result of catastrophising than an accurate assessment of the situation. The less Maria demanded of George to protect her from her insecurities, the less opportunity there was for her to hate him for failing to come through.

Beyond Separate Interests

Maria's general narrative and 'style of life' meant that every time her desires clashed with someone else's she experienced a lose-lose situation. In relation to going on holiday for example, either George got what he wanted, or she did, but either way she'd pay a price: if she said no, she'd feel guilty for not pleasing George, and if she agreed she wouldn't please herself.

In George's mind, if he got what he wanted, he won, even if Maria didn't really want to go — he had no issue with 'winning' at her expense. He was consumed by his own security needs, which involved distracting himself from feelings of helplessness and boredom. Getting Maria to do something she didn't want to do was therefore satisfying in itself: he'd feel powerful again, however on a deeper level he would feel some guilt for not considering Maria.

The only way out for a guilt-prone person in these circumstances is to see it as a win-win situation, and that can only come from reframing the choice that is in front of them. Firstly, they need to realise that no one benefits in the long run when someone disregards their own voice or what they feel is right for them. Maria's in-flight experience also provides an example of this: shortly after her forgiveness experience, George told Maria that he was feeling anxious about the plane taking off and asked for her reassurance. George was pale and clearly distressed, and miraculously Maria was happy to be there for him. George had been satisfied when he got his own way but, in the end, this didn't relieve him of the anxiety and agitation that had made him so insistent on going on a holiday in the first place.

We need to realise that the only way anyone 'wins' is to be true to themselves, which means being true to their Self. We can't necessarily stop someone from doing what they are determined to do but we don't have to sacrifice our own sense of what is right for us by going along with them. To put this into action means not to be rattled by someone's insistence that they will suffer somehow if you go against what they want. To use an analogy from the Course, even though a baby might scream and carry-on if you take a pair of scissors away from them, it doesn't mean that you're not helping them. In many cases, the most loving thing we can do for someone is to set firm boundaries. At other times, going along with someone might be the more appropriate thing to do, but only if it doesn't go against what feels right for us.

Form Versus Content

The Course emphasises the importance of distinguishing between form and content; a distinction central to its framework of forgiveness. The thirteenth-century Christian theologian and mystic Meister Eckhart provides an example of the difference between form and content in terms of what we *do* and what we *are*: 'We should not think holiness is based on what we do but rather on what we are, for it is not our works which sanctify us but we who sanctify our works'.[103]

Eckhart wasn't a Church favourite at the time of his ministry, and no doubt his emphasis on content rather than form was a contributing factor. Instead of preaching the importance of acts of penance and ritual (cornerstones of Church dogma), Eckhart emphasised the *spirit* in which we do things. In this way, anything could be a holy act — eating, sleeping or reading — and any religious ritual (such as fasting or reciting certain prayers) should be freely let go without worry if we don't find it helpful:

> *For God does not notice the nature of the works but only the love, the devotion and the spirit which is in them. For he is not so much concerned with our works as with the spirit with which we perform them all...*[104]

The emphasis isn't on the behaviour, but on the motivation for it — on the 'purity' with which it is performed.

Likewise, we can fight the good fight — work for social justice for example — but what is important is that we do it without hatred towards those we regard as the opposition. If there is hatred, then we are fighting a personal dragon — a dragon representing some aspect of ourselves that we want to deny, or a figure or situation from our past. Thus, though the form of what we are doing might come under the guise of 'caring' or 'justice', the content won't be loving nor truly helpful to ourselves or others.

The importance of the *content* of our actions is also exemplified in the following statement by one of the religious Brothers who assisted Mother Teresa in her work with the sick and dying: 'Certainly, love is expressed first in being *with* before doing *to* someone. We have to continually renew our awareness of this because we can get caught up in a lot of the doing for'.[105] So often during interactions with others, we focus on the form of their problems and want to 'fix' them, and so we are not *with* them. This is a particularly relevant point for therapists of all persuasions who can fall into the trap of focussing on the patient's problem rather than the patient themselves, thereby disengaging from them. If all our distress comes from a belief in separation, then *being with* someone first and foremost is the most important ingredient in healing.

An experience of Joanne Greenberg (Frieda Fromm-Reichmann's patient discussed in Chapter Four) illustrates the importance of this. During Joanne's time in a psychiatric hospital, her usual therapist went on leave for several weeks and was replaced by a Doctor Royson. The new doctor had impeccable logic and demanded that Joanne see the errors in her thinking. Joanne agreed with him many times — his work was clever and sometimes 'brilliant' — yet it was clear to her that all he wanted was to be right, and her sense of isolation increased.[106]

Joanne's mental health declined. Royson's emphasis on the form of the problem rather than the content created a distance between him and his patient, thus compounding her experience of loneliness and separation. Therefore, while our particular training provides a helpful context for our work, the content of our interaction (to meet someone without judgement, thereby not distancing ourselves from them; to be *with* them) is the most potent factor in healing.

Using the Course's terminology, when we're focussed on how our expertise sets us apart from someone, we are walking in front of them; when we're focussed on how someone seems to have something that we don't have, we are walking behind them. Focussing on what sets us apart in form (our education, experience, financial status, appearance, occupation, interests) is therefore a way of maintaining distance between ourselves and others.

The distinction between form and content is also relevant

considering the variety of therapies aimed at helping us feel better. One pitfall of using examples such as Maria's is that we can mistake a therapeutic technique for the healing agent itself, particularly in light of the current regard for mindfulness practice as a panacea. Healing the mind, according to the Course, always entails an inner correction whereby we no longer identify with shame and guilt, nor project them onto someone else. The result of healing is inner peace or forgiveness, and the form in which our choice for healing is expressed is simply the 'language' that we can most easily accept.

Therefore, while mindfulness can help us detach from our thoughts and relax, the true agent of Maria's peaceful (and *loving*) state was her willingness to no longer harbor anger, resentment and blame towards George, or identify with victimhood — to open her mind to the possibility that she could feel better, despite what she had accused her husband of doing. This enabled her to become receptive to her Self — to an identification with wholeness and security, and so to feel love instead of fear. Maria could therefore have had the same result listening to music, saying a prayer, taking a sedative or pressing acupressure points if those forms appealed to her as agents of healing. But the real source of her *peace* was her change of mind — this was the *content*, or *purpose*, behind her use of mindfulness.

Love or Fear

In the Course's theory, there are only two motivations or 'contents' of our behaviour — love or fear. To come from fear is to be identified with shame and guilt; to come from love is to be identified with the innocence and wholeness of our Self.

If, when filled with rage or despair over the unkind behaviour of others, we ask for Help to overcome our resentments and grievances, we'll often gain insight into the fear behind someone else's actions — whether this insight comes via something we read, see or hear. As the Course says, 'Frightened people can be vicious' (T-3.I.4:1). Even when someone says cruel things to us, they think this protects them in some way. The mythologist Joseph Campbell once suggested that instead of focussing on what someone is saying, listen to who's saying them: it's not the actual words that will tell us the most about what a person is trying to communicate, but the state of mind they appear to be in. Inspired by Help, we will hear the fear behind someone's unkindness, defensiveness, self-obsession, grandiosity, or competitiveness.

Such a shift in perception can't be achieved on our own because we are so attached to our past learning and to attributing meaning to form. Asking for Help is like making ourselves available to a sixth sense beyond the limitations of our senses and past learning. Borrowing from the English poet William Blake, we could say that with Help we're able to look *through* rather than *with* the eye:

> *This Life's dim Windows of the Soul*
> *Distorts the Heavens from Pole to Pole*
> *And leads you to Believe a Lie*
> *When you see with, not thro', the Eye* [107]

The belief in our own guilt also makes it difficult to see someone else as fearful rather than sinful, simply because we lack the motivation to do it. The popularity of newspapers is partly due to the attraction of seeing a villain *out there.* We feel let off the hook when we can label someone else as 'evil' — we're not so bad after all in comparison. I remember one of my highschool teachers talking about a newspaper dedicated to printing only good news. Unsurprisingly, it didn't sell well.

Our Shared Need

We are all different in form. We have different bodies, different personalities, different religious beliefs, and different preferences. Focussing on these differences and believing they're important is a way of affirming our separation from Oneness, ensuring our continuing identification with shame, guilt and our separate 'ego' self: 'Thoughts of essential sameness are unacceptable to the ego, because they clearly point to the non-existence of the ego itself' (T-4.V.2:2). It's not that we shouldn't embrace our individuality, quirks and preferences, but that we don't make a big deal about the differences we can perceive. We can choose to see behind our differences to our one *shared* need: to be free of our identification with shame and guilt, to remember our home and our Self. This is how we walk beside someone. We can't experience Oneness here, but its earthly reflection lies in acknowledging that we share the same essential fears and longing.

Adding to the differences we perceive between ourselves and others, are competing interests. We have different security needs based on our solutions, and these needs often conflict with the security needs of others. We also encounter competing interests in the daily commerce of life. The need of a retailer to make a profit for example competes with the need of a consumer to conserve their money. In such a situation and on the level of form, the interests of both parties do compete with each other. Seeing our shared need doesn't mean we should be naïve or self-sacrificing, but that regardless of all the posturing and bartering that goes on in form, we can still acknowledge the person we are dealing with as a brother or sister on the 'selfsame road' as ourselves.

> *Even at the level of the most casual encounter, it is possible for two people to lose sight of separate interests, if only for a moment. That moment will be enough. Salvation has come (M-3.2:6-8).*

We think our salvation comes from having our security needs met, however the true way we gain in any situation — regardless of the outcome in form — is to quietly and internally acknowledge our mutual need. Perhaps this will remind us that we don't have to argue for the sake of being right or showing off, or simply that we don't have to view someone else as 'the enemy'. Then we will do whatever we need to do for the sake of our business, family, or self, but we'll do it from a kinder place and will feel better — not because our defensive needs have been met (which may or may not be the case) but because we recognised, if only for a moment, our one shared need and in this recognition of sameness our need was answered.

Forgiveness and the Pendulum Effect

It's something of a cliché when children brought up in a strict, conservative environment go on to live a life of excess at the first opportunity they get. There's a sense of making up for lost time and rebelling over the past. Likewise, we can swing in the opposite direction, reining ourselves in to a fanatical degree, if historically we've been 'out of control'. This pendulum effect is common when we view some aspect of the way we have been as repugnant: our new, equally extreme position, is a form of overcompensation. Perhaps that's why it's said that the strictest observers of religious dogmas are often those who have converted to the faith. Asking for Help to see ourselves and others differently as we practice forgiveness is what helps to prevent this pendulum swing from occurring. Without Help to look on our solution we risk becoming repulsed by it and turning completely to its opposite.

The life of philosopher Friedrich Nietzsche provides an example of this pendulum effect. Friedrich was the son of Ludwig Nietzsche, a Lutheran pastor whose father was also a pastor. The Nietzsche clan took their religion seriously and for them life had a decidedly sombre tone. Friedrich's maternal grandfather was also a pastor, however he wasn't at all solemn. On the contrary, his lineage enjoyed the arts, music, theatre, the odd bit of gambling, and he himself was an astute and competitive businessman who made his fortune in farming. Friedrich's mother reflected this lighter approach to religion and life, and though Ludwig was a reserved man, Friedrich's upbringing was full of warmth.

Tragedy struck the family, however, when Nietzsche was five years old: Ludwig died after a year of suffering with a terminal brain disease. Friedrich had always been a pious child, but after the death of his father his religiosity went up a notch or three. When he attended primary school, his scrupulosity in obeying rules and his ability to recite biblical passages earned him the nickname 'little pastor'. Nietzsche came to embody many respects of the compliant solution. Perhaps he was imitating his father in an attempt to keep him close, but for a child his age a parent's illness or death is a very frightening scenario — with the death or unmasking of a parental god comes the realisation that there really isn't anyone who can totally take care of us; at least not always. Nietzsche's scrupulosity could therefore also have been a symptom of anxiety.

Nietzsche's love of Christianity was to undergo a radical shift in his later years at school. He began to learn critical thinking skills and applied them to his study of history and religion, questioning long-held assumptions about how life should be lived. Looking back on his early childhood he saw his father as sensitive and lovable, but also 'morbid' and without the zest of his mother. There had been no happy spark in Ludwig, the loyal servant of God who died a painful, slow death, aged only thirty-seven. Of what use was a religion that reduced life to a test of self-denial and endurance in the hope of happiness in an afterlife?

Nietzsche began to view Christianity as a harmful force that made us despise our own nature, subdue our passions and ambitions and forever rein ourselves in. He felt that having the courage to engage fully with life was noble and that we shouldn't regard what the world has to offer as evil: a noble characteristic was to say 'Yes!' to life, not to spurn and avoid it. In contrast, Christianity (according to Nietzsche) turned people into 'life-deniers'. Looking back on his life, Nietzsche felt that he had been deceived — that he had been living as an old man when he could have been enjoying life.

There is much to what Nietzsche was saying. Christianity does seem to promote the self-effacing attitude of the guilt-prone person. The problem, however, is that Nietzsche threw the baby out with the bathwater by rejecting other Christian values such as compassion, gentleness, charity and the wider-held value of social justice. According to Nietzsche, the powerless weren't in need of a helping hand but a will to strive for what they wanted, and demands for social justice are how the weak seek revenge on the powerful by trying to drag them down. There'd be no 'affirmative action' in Nietzsche's world — no attempt to make powerful institutions more representative of minorities, nor scholarships for the disadvantaged.

The ardent adoption of the polar opposite to Christian values (many of which were shared with secular society) may have contributed to the decline in Nietzsche's mental health when he was forty-four years old. Nietzsche developed an attitude of superiority and loathing toward the average person — the individual leading a life seemingly undifferentiated from the 'slavish herd'. He exalted power, health, and those who make their mark in the world. Ironically, Nietzsche himself was often ill, he was awkward and unsuccessful in his dealings with women, and his writing was generally not well received during his life. His conscious deification of the strong and powerful (along with his repulsion towards what he regarded as weakness) could be seen as a reaction to underlying feelings of inferiority.

In rejecting the compliant solution of his youth rather than forgiving the Church for some of its doctrines and himself for having adopted the solution in the first place, Nietzsche developed the attitude of its polar, negative opposite and with disastrous consequences. Nietzsche embarked on a mission to deride everything that Christianity stood for with the fervour of someone who had been burnt by it. Eventually he suffered a psychotic break with reality. Though the exact cause of Nietzsche's illness is unknown, his psychological 'one-sidedness' is likely to have played a role.

When we look without Help upon the way we have been and on those we blame for us having been that way, our sight becomes skewed and we see only the bad in what has passed. Focussing on someone or something in this way puts us on a fast track to becoming erratic and uncentred: we'll become immersed in an all-consuming anger linked to feelings of deprivation and a desire for retribution. We all find ourselves in this position from time to time but remaining in it isn't a good idea.

Importantly, simply trying to see something good in someone or something isn't the best focus — in fact, from our perspective at the time it can seem a ludicrous proposition. Instead, a more balanced view of things naturally occurs as we ask for Help and become mindful of our projections. As with the case of Maria discussed earlier, our desire to move on from the past will be met with moments of synchronicity that help us to forgive. We get exactly what we need to let go of grievances when we are ready to do so, and we'll get that help in a form that is meaningful to us. Asking for Help also avails us of the memory of our Self which assures us that we remain whole and undamaged by whatever has gone on in the past — we are trying to *realise* our wholeness, not create it.

A Fork in the Road

Almost all of us experience the same dilemma as Nietzsche at some stage in life: we look back on the way we've been living and clearly see its limitations. Nietzsche's example reflects some of the pitfalls in addressing a compliant solution. Addressing the aggressive solution is also relevant to any of us who has ever embarked on an ambitious venture, only to find ourselves questioning the very values that brought us to it in the first place. For example, we might enter a career path or adopt a role that we feel is a natural fit for us — one that we can enjoy. The problem is that — at least initially — all our roles in the world are enmeshed with a need to defend ourselves from shame and guilt. All our relationships — with people, or projects for example — begin with a large dose of neediness associated with them.

In his essay *Why I Write*, for example, George Orwell, most famous for his novels *1984* and *Animal Farm*, and someone for whom writing certainly seemed a natural fit, nonetheless listed sheer egoism — namely, a desire to seem clever, to be remembered, taken notice of, to 'show' others — as a major motive for writing in the first place.[108]

But no matter how hard we try, external validation can't make up for a shameful (or guilty) self-concept. In mistaking the problem for something that can be remedied by what we *do*, we amp up our efforts to get what constitutes success for us. In any event there comes a time when we can no longer sustain the load. We might suffer burnout or otherwise reach a crisis point. This moment can feel overwhelming, but it can also mark a transition in which we begin to question the *purpose* behind what we do.

As with the pitfalls inherent in Nietzsche's example, the risk at this stage would be to look on everything we have done in the name of success with scorn and disgust and decide that the other side of the equation is the best way to live. This scenario is central to J.D. Salinger's novella *Franny and Zooey*. Franny suffers a breakdown after concluding that her career in the theatre is tainted with 'ego', and 'phoniness' and therefore isn't worth pursuing.[109]

Franny's one-sided view of the theatre leads to her becoming extremely antagonistic towards it. She says she wants something deeper, something 'beautiful' and decides that an experience of God is the most important thing in life, and that she needs to leave the things of the world behind and concentrate on a special mantra — 'The Jesus Prayer' — to achieve this.

Zooey, Franny's brother, explains to her that the *purpose* of 'The Jesus Prayer' is what is important. There is no point, therefore, in repeating words to open the heart while simultaneously attacking and rejecting people and the world. Zooey suggests that acting in the theatre is not the problem: instead of being a form of self-aggrandisement, acting could be used as a way of extending love and kindness to others. This realisation and an acknowledgement that all people are fighting a hard battle (even those who appear to be popular or obnoxious) leads to Franny's release. She is able to forgive the theatre-world for the role it can play in self-aggrandisement, and herself for having used it for that purpose in the past. She then returns to that world with a new purpose — one in which her spiritual values and role are integrated. Many of us face the same dilemma as Franny at some stage in our lives. The challenge is not to mistake our role for the problem, rather than the purpose we have given it.

The important part that forgiveness plays in integration of the personality was brought home to me during my own process of coming to terms with my solution and its opposite. Looking back over my life I can see that I've tended towards guilt-proneness and the compliant solution. Several years ago, I felt a growing need to experience something more dynamic, though I couldn't associate this feeling with anything in particular. Around this time, I had a dream that provided a metaphor for what I needed to do in order to step into the more dynamic part of my nature.

I dreamt that I was hosting Christmas for my family but had to leave to buy a coat before serving dinner. I walked into a clothing store and looked in a mirror. The coat I was wearing was dark brown. It fitted me well and I looked okay in it, but it wasn't quite right. I selected a red coat from a rack, put it on and looked at my reflection. The colour was more pleasing but the coat was ill-fitting. A shop assistant suggested that I try a light-blue coat that was hanging from a higher rack. I noticed it was of all-natural fibre and was concerned about the cost. I looked at the price tag and was surprised that it wasn't expensive at all. Besides, it was such a beautiful blue and I knew it would fit me perfectly.

The meaning of the dream was clear when I awoke. Brown symbolised the relatively stagnant, absorbing or passive nature of the compliant solution, while red symbolised the more dynamic, fiery nature of the aggressive solution. Neither solution represented my true nature, and going from one to the other wasn't a good 'fit' for me. The blue coat of natural fibres represented communication (blue) with my higher 'natural' Self. It was such communication — achieved by asking for Help — that would enable me to forgive the fire I had judged harshly in myself and others, and all those I held responsible for my having adopted a compliant solution. I could then express the positive counterparts of both fire and absorption: love-inspired action and receptivity. The significance of Christmas in the dream points to the correlation between the rebirth of our Self (associated with Christ) and the rebirth of our *whole* personality.

Alchemy — the ancient art of chemical transformation — also illustrates the need for requesting Help of a transcendent order when trying to move on from our solutions. The alchemists were chemists interested in the kind of transformation that occurs when two chemical opposites are combined, a gentle heat applied, and the vapour distilled. The resulting substance would seem vastly different to the original constituents. The alchemists noticed that it was through such 'reconciliation of opposites' (the process of recalling our projections) that major transformation also occurred in people, but they also noticed that the meeting of opposites alone didn't lead to transformation but only to increased conflict. In alchemy, the two opposites are combined in the presence of mercury — an otherworldly substance that is neither a solid nor a liquid. Mercury represents the Help we call on to see others and ourselves differently; a bridge to the spiritual dimension of our Self and the facilitator of forgiveness.

The choice between self-effacement and self-aggrandisement, or between self-sacrifice and winning seems to be *the* choice that we have to make day in and day out. Nietzsche took issue with Christianity for seeming to glorify the weak and submissive while demonising the powerful. The other side of the argument is that choosing self-interest leaves the welfare of others in its wake. Amongst all the choices that the world seems to offer, if we are identified with the ego-thought system we are only ever really choosing between these alternatives — identifying with guilt or with shame, victim or victimiser. Guilt demands that we must deny ourselves the pleasures of the world in order to atone; shame demands that we prove our worth by accumulating wordly power and recognition.

Oliver Sacks wrote an open letter to *The New York Times* leading up to his death (in 2015) in which he said that though he wasn't without fear, his predominant feeling was one of gratitude — that he had been given much and given something in return: he had had an intercourse with the world through his writing and reading.[110] I love this idea of 'communing' with the world: instead of seeking to find happiness in the things of the world or recoiling from the world as something dangerous, we could aim to have a dialogue with it — to have an exchange that enriches us both.

A genuine alternative to being a 'hammer or anvil' is to choose the wholeness of our Self. The way in which this choice is expressed is to meet the day with the intention of observing our judgements and practicing forgiveness. Not only do we have old issues that cause distress, but we also have daily encounters that seem to battle us for our peace. The likelihood that we will encounter someone rude or thoughtless during our day may be high, but these daily irritants provide us with an opportunity to address our own issues. If we have identified with shame or guilt, we are likely to respond to setbacks in our circumstances or the way others behave with strong feelings of being persecuted and deprived. But we have agency: we're not the playthings of God or circumstance. All power lies within our minds to choose whether or not we will bring our perceptions, judgments, grievances and self-concept into question. We are being 'authentic' whenever we relate to ourselves as having this power to choose.

Resistance

> *It is a long-superseded idea... that the patient suffers from a sort of ignorance, and that if one removes this ignorance by giving him information (about the causal connection of his illness with his life, about his experiences in childhood, and so on) he is bound to recover. The pathological factor is not his ignorance in itself, but the root of this ignorance in his inner resistances.*[111]
>
> Sigmund Freud

Though the process leading to forgiveness may sound simple, it is far from easy. This is because our self-concept is bound to the shame and guilt we long to be rid of: we are so identified with our solutions, that letting them go (and the past associated with them) can feel like we're losing a fundamental part of ourselves. We therefore resist looking at (let alone letting go of) our habitual ways of being and perceiving. Indeed, so strong is our resistance to questioning our current beliefs and grievances that we are prone to attack anything or anyone that challenges them, which is precisely what happened to Socrates.

Socrates' way of helping others approach Truth was to pose questions that helped them recognise errors in their thinking that obscured their connection to Truth. These usually involved notions of justice, courage, success, kindness and morality. Where people thought their beliefs were rationally sound, Socrates exposed their inconsistencies. Artfully stripped of ideas they had assumed were correct, those on the receiving end of Socrates' questions would find themselves in a state of uncertainty, and they generally didn't like it. Though this more open state of mind is the gateway to an intuitive grasp of the Self, we can experience it as deeply unsettling. For Socrates' accusers especially, the link between their beliefs and their self-concept was acutely felt, and Socrates' questioning threatened the self they thought they were, with tragic consequences for Socrates.

Even once we have willingly begun questioning our judgements, resistance can continue to play a part. Our attachment to our self-concept as we've known it is why letting go of our shame and guilt can be painful: not only can we feel that something precious is being taken away from us, but metaphorically having one foot on the accelerator to move on and the other on the brake because of our resistance induces a great deal of strain. It's important to realise the discomfort involved in addressing our ego, and to appreciate the diligence, commitment and fortitude required to fully engage with any authentic spiritual path. To expect that looking at our grievances and asking for Help will rid us of our shame and guilt in a day, a week or a decade is to again mistake forgiveness for a magic trick.

Resistance is familiar to long-term adherents of a spiritual path or psychological inquiry. Despite many years of study and application, we might wonder why we still act in self-defeating ways, or respond to someone's angry outburst with an equally aggressive defensiveness, though fully aware of the mechanics of projection. In the end, what allows healing to occur is our *willingness* to be free of the past and the shame and guilt associated with it. Developing this willingness takes time. The best way of dealing with our resistance is to gently observe it and accept that when our fear of letting go of a grievance has lessened, we will be free of it: we need to be patient with ourselves and recognise the depth of the process we have begun and respect our own timing. In honouring, rather than over-emphasising our resistance, we help to soften it — crucially, we are not making our reluctance to let go of 'the devil we know' a 'sin'; yet another thing to feel guilty about.

In short, it takes a long time for us to become willing to let go of our solutions, grievances and associated self-concepts because we're not sure we'd be better off without them. Moving beyond our issues is therefore a matter of trust. An acceptance that letting go of our solutions will give us safety, peace and joy is something we grow into, and this is why our work with forgiveness can be characterised as *the development of trust.*

The Development of Trust

A Course in Miracles describes the development of trust as a six-stage process. Like Kubler-Ross's stages of grief, they aren't meant to be taken as a description of what *everyone* goes through, and although they are presented in a sequential fashion, there can be much toing and froing between them. As with everything else in life, 'the map is not the territory' — there's only so much that any theory can describe. That being said, the following stages are helpful in giving context to some common experiences encountered as we develop trust that practicing forgiveness will give us what we truly want.

Stage One: A Period of Undoing

The first stage in the development of trust involves questioning the idea that our happiness depends on what goes on around us. We learn that our intense emotions are the result of our *interpretations* of events, not the events themselves. This is a huge shift in emphasis from what goes on around us to what goes on in our mind, and at first we're likely to resist entertaining the idea that this is true in all circumstances: 'This is the truth, at first to be but said and then repeated many times; and next to be accepted as but partially true, with many reservations. Then to be considered seriously more and more, and finally to be accepted as truth' (W-284).

This stage is painful because the motivation to make this major shift in thinking often comes via a difficult external circumstance, such as a sudden job loss or relationship crisis, that challenges our sense of security and worthiness. These are the 'inescapable circumstances' discussed in Chapter Five which bring up issues surrounding shame and guilt. When we can no longer manipulate circumstances to protect us from our deepest fears, we must look at those fears directly: our orientation shifts from the outer world to the inner.

Moving through this stage involves stretching beyond the dictates of our solution, and practicing forgiveness helps us do this. We begin to realise that we don't *need* whatever crutch we relied on in the past to feel secure. We begin to trust in the idea that the world doesn't rule the mind. When we have learned that any circumstance can be helpful to us as a means of forgiveness — of letting go of shame and guilt — we go on to the second stage.

Stage Two: A Period of Sorting Out

Generalisation is the challenge of this stage: we need to accept that the only valuable thing about *all* circumstances is the opportunity to become aware of our projected shame and guilt (expressed in our judgements of others) and to remember our one shared need. Here our fear of letting go of our solution — of our habitual means for feeling pleasure and avoiding pain — will make us reluctant to question our judgements and habitual responses in *every* circumstance. We might only be willing to practice forgiveness in a few situations — with a work colleague but not with our partner, for example — but as we continue to practice, the results will increase our trust and motivation to really put the Course principles into practice in *all* situations.

As we accept that the major value in any relationship or circumstance is to practice forgiveness, we learn to regard all interactions as equally valuable because of the developmental purpose they can serve. This is another major shift: we are strongly bound to believing that some encounters/people are more important to us than others because we believe that some *offer* us more than others. We might, for example, think a close association with someone famous improves our status in the world and so offers us a lot. In contrast, interacting with a 'regular' stranger mightn't seem to offer us much at all.

Stage Three: A Period of Relinquishment

Having accepted that the most valuable thing in any circumstance is the opportunity to address shame, guilt and recognise our shared need, the next stage is to let go of the motivations that have driven us in the past. Here again we experience pain and conflict, this time because we feel that we're asked to sacrifice our own best interests. We think we *need* to strive for status or success (shame-prone), or to self-sacrifice (guilt-prone), in order to provide for our own safety and happiness. At this stage, we need to decide what we will align ourselves with: the thought system associated with our defensive solutions or with forgiveness.

About halfway through my Rolfing career the need for me to make this decision became clear. I'd felt that there was something missing in my work but couldn't put a finger on it. Around the same time, I decided that I'd like to try my hand at writing and publishing a professional paper. I had been drawn to the issue of chronic hamstring strain (interesting to some!) and wanted to integrate what I had learnt from several perspectives into a cohesive model. The paper was accepted into a peer-reviewed journal and when it was finally published, I was excited to see it cited by researchers abroad. To my disappointment however, this momentary spark of enthusiasm didn't remain and I still felt discontented with my practice. I couldn't work out what to do. Did I need to do some hands-on continuing education to revitalise my work?

As is often the case when the conscious mind struggles to define a problem (let alone come up with a solution), I received some insight from a dream: I was seated opposite a doctor in their office. Curiously, the doctor was a person I had met in my waking life and whom I had judged harshly. She said to me kindly but firmly, 'You need to decide what you want to do'.

'It's Rolfing, isn't it?' I said.

'Yes, but it doesn't give you a zing. That's why you've got that sore throat'. I had felt fine physically up until this point, but now became aware that my throat was indeed sore.

'What did I come here for?' I asked, confused as to why I was there.

'Itchy feet', she replied. I then woke up, with a sore throat.

The doctor was telling me that it was time to decide whether I wanted to follow the ego's path for happiness — to focus on the achievement of worldly success and status — or the Course's path of forgiveness (which is why the doctor appeared as someone I needed to forgive). The zing I wasn't getting from Rolfing related to how I was using it, the sore throat was symbolic of my resistance to communicating with my Self which would naturally entail truly 'communing' with others. Fortunately, I listened to the dream and made a conscious decision to make forgiveness and truly *being with* my clients the goal of my work. I continued to employ the techniques and theory I was well versed in, I just did this from a different mindset. And almost immediately my work began to be rewarding in ways I never imagined. Most notably, I found that *being with* my clients was far more healing for all concerned than simply trying to fix them.

Stage three can therefore be seen as a time in which we decide resolutely to plant our flag in a philosophy of life that establishes our goal as inner peace and accepts forgiveness as the means to obtain it.

Stage Four: A Period of Settling Down

The challenge in the first three stages of the development of trust is to have faith that the process of forgiveness gives us what we truly want, and that every circumstance provides us with this opportunity — that, in fact, it is this opportunity that makes an encounter meaningful. By stage four we've learnt that the world doesn't have the power to take away our peace and there is comfort in the knowledge that we don't walk alone. We still have moments of distress, but we notice that their intensity and duration aren't what they used to be, and we settle into what the Course refers to as a period of 'reasonable' happiness and peace.

This stage isn't as painful as the ones that precede it — in fact, it contains many moments of real happiness — so much so that we can believe we've made it to the other side of our ego. Perhaps the most important aspect of this stage is that it provides us with a store of memories to draw on for strength and faith during the next and hardest stage — a 'period of unsettling' in which everything seems to be going wrong.

9

The Dark Night of the Soul

We enter stage five in our development of trust when we become dissatisfied with reasonable happiness and, on some level, say yes to addressing the remnants of shame and guilt that obscure our Self. Experiencing the shame and guilt at the core of our self-concept is deeply painful, as is looking at their origins. In stage five, not only are we approaching the 'beginning' of our shame and guilt in terms of our personal history and authority problems with our parents, but — whether we have an intellectual acceptance of this or not — we are also getting closer to our imagined authority problem with God, and this adds to our distress. As the following passage from Evelyn Underhill's book *Mysticism* highlights, the path to knowledge of our Self is not without significant trials:

> *No transmutation without fire, say the alchemists: No cross, no crown, says the Christian. All the great experts of the spiritual life agree — whatever their creeds, their symbols, their explanations — in describing this stress, tribulation, and loneliness, as an essential part of the way from the Many to the One; bringing the self to the threshold of that*

> *completed life which is to be lived in intimate union with Reality.*[112]

Resistance again plays a significant role in our pain at this stage: we fear losing the self we have identified with and sought refuge in for so long — a self linked to our solutions. To question and let go of our identification with shame, guilt and the past is therefore like contemplating our death. This is why the Course talks of our *attraction* to guilt — who would we be without our problems and grievances? Who would we be without our past? So, while by this stage we're more peaceful and kinder than we were in the past, we're still attached to the 'I' we think we are. At stage five we address this attachment more directly.

In Buddhism, the 'I' of the false ego-self is that which craves some things and is repulsed by others, and freedom lies in raising the mind above desire and loathing. Likewise, when we are identified with our ego, we are identified with shame and guilt; the source of all strong emotional investments and neediness. In other words, if we're not craving or loathing something, we're not identifying with our ego and our mind is free of the tyranny of the 'shoulds' and 'musts'. One way of noticing how attached we still are to our ego, therefore, is to see how much we still want to be admired, desired, approved of, preferred or respected, and how fearful we are of being forgotten, rejected, ridiculed, abandoned or attacked.

It's these remnants of desire and loathing that are the target of the cleansing process of stage five. Our emotional investments maintain a focus on the world as a source of pleasure and pain and holding onto them is way of denying that 'there is no peace except the peace of God' (W-200). To borrow an analogy from Saint John of the Cross, just as a bird tied to a branch by five strings is still bound if four strings are cut, we too are bound to our ego until we truly make forgiveness (the peace of God; remembrance of our Self) *the most important thing* in our lives and are willing to let go of *all* our grievances.

This is how we cut the final string. We will still have ego thoughts, but we will no longer be bound by them because we've placed our mind well and truly in the service of forgiveness. Reflecting the words of the nineteenth century Indian saint Sri Ramakrishna, when we are willing to practice forgiveness we might still identify as 'I', but it is an 'I' no longer at the mercy of passions because it is in the service of God:

> *Very few can get rid of the sense of 'I' through samadhi [meditation]. It generally clings to us. We may discriminate a thousand times, but the sense of 'I' is bound to return again and again... If this sense of 'I' will not leave, then let it stay on as the servant of God... If this attitude of a servant be genuine and perfect, then passion and anger will drop off leaving only a scar in the mind.*[113]

Stage five is analogous to what Saint John of the Cross called 'The Dark Night of the Spirit'. The more familiar term —The Dark Night of the *Soul* — actually consists of two types of 'nights' (each of which can last years): The Dark Night of the *Senses*; and the Dark Night of the *Spirit*. We first encounter the Dark Night of the Senses when we realise that the world itself has nothing to offer us in the way of true comfort, security or meaning. We experience the futility of looking to power and status, or self-sacrifice and romantic love, or resigned detachment, for our happiness, and so things seem to darken. We then begin looking inward rather than outward for the source of both our pain and our comfort. In terms of the Course it's also a time when we begin to address our projections of shame and guilt through the process of forgiveness, and can be likened to the first three stages in the development of trust.

The Dark Night of the *Spirit* is about truly relinquishing our investment in the 'I, me, mine' of the ego-self, and uniting with our Self: 'Now must you choose between yourself and an illusion of yourself. Not both, but one' (T-22.II.6:1, 6-9). As we enter this night, our commitment to forgiveness isn't yet total because we're not sure of what will be waiting for us when we let go of the past. That's why it's important to have had some intimation of the happiness that awaits us on the other side of our ego, to give us the faith and motivation to carry us through this extremely testing time. Since the Dark Night of the Spirit is most commonly referred to as the Dark Night of the Soul, I've used 'Soul' instead of 'Spirit' in the following discussion for the sake of clarity.

The Experience

The Dark Night of the Soul is marked by an absence of spiritual consolation. Saint John portrays the Dark Night as a time of great spiritual aridity when compared to the relative abundance of 'spiritual feeling' we experienced in earlier stages. He describes how the pleasure we gained before from 'sweet meditations' and good works now alludes us. Things that used to help in desperate moments no longer seem to work and trying to put them into practice only leads to frustration and confusion — aren't we doing what the Course/our spiritual practice suggests? We can feel that we have taken a huge step backwards, rather than in fact moving forwards:

> *And thus He leaves them so completely in the dark that they know not whither to go with their sensible imagination and meditation; for they cannot advance a step in meditation, as they were wont to do aforetime, their inward senses being submerged in this night, and left with such dryness that not only do they experience no pleasure and consolation in the spiritual things and good exercises wherein they were wont to find their delights and pleasures, but instead, on the contrary, they find insipidity and bitterness in the said things... everything seems to be going wrong with them.*[114]

Though we enter the Dark Night gradually, feeling that we can't connect as before to what is 'spiritual', once both feet are fully in the Dark Night of the Soul we experience a rapid descent into a darkness that is confounding. Along with a sense of helplessness, we feel totally and utterly unworthy. It's as if God, the Universe, or whatever you like to call That which Knows and Loves, has withdrawn from us, leaving behind an overwhelming sense of darkness, deprivation and inner poverty. And not only do we feel deprived of Love, we can also experience an absence of any longing for it.

Emptiness and aridity are therefore the dominant aspects of our experience. Indeed, it is this spiritual aridity — feeling ourselves, the world and our spiritual aspirations to be empty — that is a major factor distinguishing the Dark Night of the Soul from 'simply' clinical depression, though they can occur together. Indeed, a defining feature of the Dark Night of the Soul is a *crisis of faith*. It's not uncommon for people who've had a natural inclination to believe in God to find themselves in the deeply disconcerting (to put it mildly) position of questioning His very existence.

Like other thresholds that herald a significant internal shift, the Dark Night of the Soul will often involve a change in external circumstances which brings up the shame and guilt we need to clear, along with potent issues related to our parents or other significant authority figures in our lives. (And as always, we are prone to project these issues onto our partners, so they may also be involved in the profound shifts at hand). Preceding the external change, we might have dreams which indicate an emotional hit is imminent: dreams of being engulfed by water, for example, or of fleeing from tidal waves. We're also likely to experience a growing sense of dissatisfaction or uneasiness that we find difficult to pin down. Is it our work? Our relationship? Our finances? Is it (as a 'good Course student' is bound to ask) that we've become lax in applying the principles of forgiveness?

This uneasiness may be followed by a growing realisation that something needs to change in our external life. However, this will often involve being willing to let go of the familiar (a relationship or job, for example) without any clear sense of what will follow: there is no sense of safety when facing the force of change. Without a clear sense of what will come next, our deepest recurring fears surrounding our self-worth and security (Will we ever find a lifelong partner? What will we do for money? What does the future hold?) meet us head on and we may experience intense anxiety and depression. To outsiders, these changes might not seem dramatic, but to the person going through them, they have particular symbolic value regarding their self-concept, history, and solution.

As we finally decide to let go of whatever crutch we had to protect us from the dregs of our shame and guilt, the sudden plunge into anxiety and despair can feel like a rug has been pulled from under us. With nothing external to give us value or justify our existence, all our misgivings about ourselves come to the fore. We're likely to question everything about ourselves — our value, our ability to go on in the world — and to fear rejection from those closest to us.

Importantly, our inner turbulence isn't a sign of regression or lack of resilience. It's an indicator that we have said yes to an even greater break with the past, and this requires looking at the darkness beneath our facades. Not everyone goes through such an intense stage of inner turbulence during their life, however this is more a function of time than 'health'. As mysticism scholar Evelyn Underhill put it:

> *The long quiet work of adjustment which others must undertake before any certitude rewards them is for these concentrated into one violent shattering and rearranging of the self, which can now begin its true career of correspondence with the Reality it has perceived.*[115]

In other words, though the goal of Self-realisation is for all, the process of attaining it is more condensed and intense for some. The problem is that we are so used to judging success and failure based on form and the world's standards that, as the Course says, we don't know the difference between advance and retreat (T-18.V.1:5).

Because others may not perceive the desolation in our external circumstances, we can suffer a profound sense of isolation. We can also feel strangely distant from ourselves, perhaps because our self-concept is being shaken at its core. Other symptoms are similar to those of thresholds generally: obsession and worry over (benign) bodily sensations and symptoms (hypochondriasis); harsh thoughts towards ourselves or others that seem to come out of nowhere ('thought intrusions'); and unusually intense moments of anger and anxiety.

Many of these symptoms were described by Saint John of the Cross in reference to his experience of the Dark Night. For example, he spoke of tremendous surges of hatred and grievances rising up within him along with 'blasphemies':

> *At other times in this night there is added to these things the spirit of blasphemy, which roams abroad, setting in the path of all the conceptions and thoughts of the soul intolerable blasphemies. These it sometimes suggests to the imagination with such violence that the soul almost utters them, which is a grave torment to it.*[116]

Though Saint John mightn't have seen it this way, when we say yes to developing trust and faith, we are also saying yes to being more of who we are, so the shame, guilt, and associated anger and sorrow come to the fore to be cleared.

An awareness that our symptoms are strange, along with the distress they cause us, indicates that our sense of self — though it may feel precarious — is intact enough to get us through. In other words, we are able to maintain just enough distance from the intensity of our inner experience to observe it rather than be lost in it. We can of course still seek help through whatever is meaningful to us. It's important, however, to realise that the pain is something we can't avoid or remove altogether as we move through the Dark Night.

Part of the pain during this time can be from uncertainty about what lies ahead. As mentioned earlier, the Dark Night can accompany a significant change in our circumstances, and we mightn't be able to see the forest for the trees for a while: life seems to present a problem for which there seems no way out. The 'unsolvable problem' is a common feature of the Dark Night. Up until this time, we've been used to defining problems and fixing them in our own way, but now we can't. On top of this, our daily routines seem more taxing, our thinking more confused and our responsibilities more demanding, particularly during the early stage of transition.

This time of uncertainty can seem hopeless but it's also a gift — it opens us up to letting go of our need to control things. It's therefore a turning point when we finally say, 'I really can't see how to fix this and I don't know what to do'. Through our humility our mind is finally open and receptive to being guided. Thus, the Dark Night of the Soul is about learning to align our will with God's — something we can't do until we're motivated to listen.

A Matter of Will

> *In the stress and anguish of the Night... the self loses the power to Do; and learns to surrender its will to the operation of a larger Life, that it may Be.*[117]
>
> Evelyn Underhill

As we've seen, the most intense part of the Dark Night (as with all major thresholds of change) is the beginning, which can last months. It's an experience of spiritual shipwreck in which we experience the most pain, doubt and fear. This is the period when our usual spiritual practices and de-stressing activities seem ineffectual, and it's best to let them go for a while rather than cling to them as a means of staving off the darkness.

Western culture places a high prize on what we can achieve through sheer willpower and determination. A gold medal at the Olympics after years of rigorous training and hardship, a grand house wrangled into existence despite substantial financial and logistical setbacks — these are the kind of things that generally constitute success stories according to our culture. The difficulty with the Dark Night is that you can't *will* or force it along. You can't make yourself 'better' quicker through sheer willpower or a combative attitude to 'beat' your darkness.

This is an important consideration in today's emphasis on evidence-based therapy. That a particular type of counselling can generally produce desirable results in six-to-eight sessions, can lead both patient and therapist to think they're doing something wrong if there's no significant improvement within a few weeks or months. Likewise, the promise of many New Age techniques to have you feeling better quicker is equally problematic during this stage. The message of the mystics is that you can't make the transition happen any faster. Jung and the mystics showed that just because there is conflict doesn't mean there is something wrong, and we need to endure the pain and uncertainty, though this is contrary to our culture's ideals.

In realising that we can't do anything to totally extricate us from our pain or speed things up, we're apt to feel that letting go of our *striving* is like laying down to die. Old habits die hard. During the morning of life, we rely heavily on our own problem-solving skills and ingenuity to get through school, work and relationships. We can therefore be reluctant to relinquish some control and trust that we needn't rely solely on our problem-solving abilities. We fear that without a fixed goal and determination we'll be left floundering without any support in the world. However, the intensity of our inner turmoil during this time is such that we eventually *have* to let go of the idea of speeding things up through one means or another. It can become extremely difficult to put our mind to anything that requires much intellectual effort.

Jung for example was unable to read a scientific book during his Dark Night after the split from Freud, and the activities he did engage in were more about *coping* with the process rather than trying to hurry it along. He found that simple, grounding activities such as playing with stones (reminiscent of his childhood), rudimentary gardening, working with stone, and cooking, helped keep himself anchored while his inner world was in a flux. Likewise, we might find talking to a therapist or taking medication to be of vital assistance in getting through this time. Again — it's not *what* we do, but the *purpose* behind it that is important. Everyone's path of forgiveness is different: as the Course emphasises, the 'curriculum' for letting go of shame and guilt is highly individualised, and this includes the form of external help we will be attracted to.

It's not uncommon, for example, for people who have grown up with a sense of stigma towards medication (and therefore a subtle judgement of those who use it) to find themselves in a situation where they are actually grateful for it — a powerful lesson that 'there is nothing either good or bad, but thinking makes it so'. Whatever we do for comfort, it's important to take it lightly — not to make a big deal about the form (medication, yoga, reading, counselling) — but to focus on the purpose of it as helping us stay afloat and work through our forgiveness lessons.

So, in the words of Saint Teresa of Avila, it's better to 'embrace the Cross' in a spirit of acceptance than to try and fight our way out of the Dark Night, and what helps us do this is being able to place our experience within its proper context. The Dark Night is a transformational process that we can't manipulate through our will. Transforming a lump of clay into a work of art relies on the vision and actions of the sculptor from start to finish. But the Dark Night is not the time for trying to mould ourselves into shape. Instead, the 'passive' transformational process related to the Dark Night is more akin to the fermentation process. When you leave grape juice for a period of time, it becomes cloudy and putrid, but if you allow the fermentation process to continue it begins to clarify and becomes wine. Likewise, our choice to become who we are and move beyond 'reasonable happiness' sets the transformation process in motion, plunging us into a fetid darkness of self-confrontation, but it is our passiveness, or rather our 'active receptivity', that allows the time and space for our inner experience to be gradually transformed into a more vital one. And that active receptivity will play its role in helping us to work through our issues — forgiveness, in the end, is the clarifying agent.

Another way of framing the process of the Dark Night and the darkening of the senses and the intellect, is to see what has been foremost in our experience recede to the background, and that which has been in the background come to the fore. Paraphrasing the Course, we let our No.1 personality step back so our No.2 personality can lead the way (W-155). During the Dark Night we have to let the intellectual control of our No.1 personality recede to let us experience the depths of our unconscious where both our fears and our No.2 personality, or Self, lie hidden. Jung, for example, felt that he had lived out his No.1 personality up until he was thirty-eight — near the onset of his Dark Night — and that he was then ready for the 'greater' No.2 personality to be integrated with it.[118]

There is, therefore, a type of surrender that's called for in the Dark Night of the Soul. And though the awakening of the inner, spiritual No.2 personality is ushered in with a crisis in which we feel utterly impotent, the strength of our reasoning and of all our faculties will return and be more dependable than in the past because they will be serving our Self.

The Sense of Sin

> *It is a great surprise to a soul that thinks itself far advanced towards perfection to see itself thus despoiled all at once.*[119]
>
> Madame Guyon

Many people find the word 'sin' disturbing because of its religious connotations, namely that we are lowly creatures in need of redemption. 'Lord, I am not worthy to receive you', are words the congregation speaks in preparation for communion in a Catholic service. Understandably, some people who were brought up with this concept of sinfulness turn away from the Church because it simply doesn't seem healthy or helpful to reinforce the idea — particularly in children — that they are unworthy and flawed. Words such as 'Universe', 'The All', or 'Love' are therefore adopted to replace the Biblical God of judgement and to distance ourselves from the concept of sin.

From the point of view of the Course, we're correct in rejecting the idea that we are inherently unworthy and sinful, along with the picture of God as a judgemental parent capable of anger and retribution. The problem is that deep down we still believe it — the archetypal scenario of a Fall is imbedded in our psyche.

When we reach our lowest points in life, whether our habit is to turn to the Universe, God, or the Dharma, we are hit with feelings of abandonment and punishment, shame and guilt, and all the fears we usually associate with the idea of God as Judge, ready to condemn: 'Why has the Universe abandoned me? What am I doing wrong'?

The sense of sin is something we commonly encounter in the Dark Night of the Soul along with an acute awareness of how bound to shame and guilt we still are. Where in stage four we thought we had transcended our poor, ego-based self-concept, we now see how much of what we did was still motivated by a desire to be special. Along with this awareness is a feeling of sinfulness. This is hard to define: it mightn't be tied up with anything in particular but it is bound to a profound sense of unworthiness far more bitter and pervasive than anything we've endured previously.

During my version of the Dark Night, feelings of sinfulness took me by surprise. After many years of working with the Course and practicing forgiveness, an unprecedented sense of sin hit me. I was brought up Catholic and this had influenced my idea of God, but I thought I'd left the concept of a punitive Father behind in my teenage years. It became clear in my Dark Night, however, that I hadn't. The God of judgement was still with me, as was acute feelings of unworthiness. Fortunately, I had a book a friend had bought for me on a whim several years before, which up until now I'd only given a cursory glance. It contained selected writings of the fourteenth-century Christian mystic Meister Eckhart, and I gravitated toward it in my distress. The words that consoled me most related to God's forgiveness of 'sinners':

> *If he finds that we are now ready [to turn to Him in repentance], then he does not consider what we were before. God is a god of the present. He takes you and receives you as he finds you now, not as you have been, but as you are now.*[120]

> *For the more inadequate and guilty we perceive ourselves to be, the more reason we have to bind ourselves to God with an undivided love, who knows neither sin nor inadequacy.*[121]

With my sense of 'old-fashioned sin' came a need for 'old-fashioned' writing about God, but not the God of judgement — it was the mystics I was turning to. The unconscious weight of sin — which ultimately comes from our belief in separation from God but is reflected in specific aspects of shame and guilt associated with our personal history — is lifted as we feel fully accepted by someone or something despite our feelings of unworthiness. At first, however, such acceptance can elicit a great deal of pain in recognition of what we'd always longed for but thought was lost — our holiness.

An illustration of this is found in Clarissa Dickson Wright's autobiography, *Spilling the Beans*. Clarissa was one of the Two Fat Ladies in the British cooking television series of that name, popular in the 1990s. Clarissa's childhood was marked with domestic violence and before her fame she was addicted to alcohol and had periods of homelessness. Eventually she began attending a twelve-step program for addiction, despite being very hostile towards others during group sessions. She described her mental and verbal defences as having a 'pit bull' physicality, but when a fellow attendee said he thought Clarissa was a *very nice person*, she burst into tears; later crying for what seemed like weeks, releasing all the pain of her life.[122]

The theme of redemption from a guilt and shame-filled self-concept was also strikingly portrayed in Robert Bolt's novel *The Mission,* where Captain Mendoza — a former mercenary, now repentant and a broken man — cries inconsolably when treated with kindness by a member of a tribe he had viciously persecuted. His tears reflected remorse for his previous lack of compassion towards others and his appreciation for being deemed worthy of kindness. There is a profound experience of gratitude when you realise that despite how much you push others away — which ultimately means pushing Love and your Self away — you are still welcome Home. *Always.* It is this archetypal, religious theme that provides the potency of our experience and the depth of our gratitude.

When we have passed through our lowest point and regain some equilibrium (very much a *relative* term at this time!) we'll find we're able to return to whatever means have helped us de-stress in the past, but without the expectation that they remove all of our pain. In terms of *A Course in Miracles,* we need to trust that if we ask for Help to look at our daily thoughts of judgement, we will get through. The process of forgiveness doesn't mean we don't *do* anything in relation to our issues. Most likely, as discussed in earlier chapters, it means stretching beyond the dictates of our solutions to face our fear of assertiveness or of emotional vulnerability and dependency, or of meaningful engagement. To know when, where and how to stretch requires receptivity to our Self and this is facilitated by asking for Help.

That Special Person

Behind Clarissa's feelings of unworthiness lay a difficult and hostile relationship with her father, deceased at the time of her writing. Arthur Dickson Wright, a renowned surgeon, was a violent alcoholic who physically and verbally abused his wife and four children. Clarissa began to hate her father when she — at age six — first witnessed him hitting her mother. From then on Arthur assumed a central place in Clarissa's life: her antagonism towards him influenced her interests and choice of career, for example. Arthur had wanted her to become a physician like himself, so Clarissa purposefully decided to study law instead.

Likewise, it is common for us have one 'special' person toward whom we hold the most anger and feelings of victimisation — a significant authority figure from the past (usually a parent) we hold responsible for our current difficulties (both inner and outer) as well as those long gone. It is our feelings of deprivation, unfair punishment and neglect at the hands of this person that hold our fear of God in place because he or she is His symbolic representative. The voice of our inner critic is the internalised voice of God and His earthly stand-in: the pressure, the 'shoulds' and 'oughts', the harassment over our imperfections all come courtesy, first and foremost, of this 'special' relationship.

Practicing forgiveness towards this person — addressing our shame and guilt in relation to them — is therefore a potent means of addressing our feelings of abandonment and punishment in relation to God. We can't let go of our fear of God nor experience peace while we hold on to our judgements because judgement implies we have identified with shame and guilt ourselves. Holding on to our anger toward this person is therefore how we hold on to our ego. Would we condemn him or her for their actions stemming from a shameful and guilty self-concept? The Course makes it clear that to condemn them is to condemn ourselves: 'should *one* brother dawn upon your sight as wholly worthy of forgiveness, then your concept of yourself is wholly changed. Your "evil" thoughts have been forgiven with his' (T-31.VII.2:5-6).

The way we lessen our fear of God is to work on releasing our shame and guilt associated with our personal history, particularly in relation to our parents and the special person. And in order to step into the authority of our Self, we need to let go of our dependency on our parents to be like gods, and to forgive them for having the common failings of humanity. As Jung wrote, psychological and spiritual growth entails no longer 'mythologizing' our parents, though we usually do this far into adulthood, and experience great resistance to stopping.[123]

Nonetheless, because our parents take on a God-like image to us as small children, part of stepping into the authority of our Self is to review this concept. This involves making a genuine break with the past and the neediness we have felt towards our parents which is projected onto other individuals such as our partners, teachers, doctors and bosses. Stepping into the authority and wholeness of our spiritual Self can only come from identifying first and foremost as a 'child of God'; practicing forgiveness is the way we do this.

The importance of the 'parentage' issue to our quest for fulfilment is expressed in myths where the protagonist goes in search of their father whom they have never known. Mythologist Joseph Campbell pointed out that the meeting of the hero with the father is about accepting our true inheritance as a child of the Eternal: the child being our earthly aspect, our 'No.1 personality', and the father representing our eternal Self.[124]

In Chapter Five we saw that a need to go in a direction counter to the path or wishes of our parents is a sign of being on the threshold of major inner change. There is, however, an important irony in the establishment of our psychological independence and following our own way: we begin to embody significant positive aspects of each parent, combined in our own unique, authentic form of self-expression. This is the concept behind alchemy — that two opposite substances are brought together and produce a third substance that is different from each constituent yet somehow reminiscent of them.

In relation to forgiveness, as we forgive our parents for the shortcomings we perceived in them, we are able to accept and integrate their positive aspects within ourselves. And, relationships being what they are, our parents are likely to lie at different places along the 'compliant-aggressive' continuum. As we forgive them for the ways in which we felt let down, unappreciated, hurt or abused, we begin to embody more of our wholeness (love-inspired action and receptivity), and this is often expressed in some mysterious way in the path that we choose. It's mysterious because it just settles upon us without conscious deliberation. As we remove the blocks of shame and guilt associated with polar opposites, we naturally express the wholeness of what Jung calls the 'irrational third' — an interest or direction that emerges from deep within, beyond the contrived analysis and planning of our conscious mind.

Moving through the Dark Night is a slow and gradual process of recalibration, the resolution of which will often be experienced as a birth of positive, expansive feeling towards an interest or activity that gives expression to an aspect of ourselves that has been liberated. What we might have previously toyed with in our minds but disregarded now begins to hold strong appeal for us. Ultimately, we have discovered a more appropriate means for expressing our own voice — our own way — and for getting in touch with our inner, loving Authority — the source of our most fulfilling expression. Where before the world seemed fallow and we wished to turn away from it, we now happily become re-engaged from a different orientation — that of our Self. The process of releasing shame and guilt is therefore redemptive, leading to a sense of rebirth and renewal along with true independence from the past.

A Personal Renaissance

The 'irrational third', or the way in which a newfound sense of wholeness and independence is conveyed, will also express the growth in integration between our No.1 and No.2 personalities — our internal, spiritual life with our external world and intellectual self. The life of author C.S. Lewis (best known for *The Narnia Chronicles*) is an example of this. Like Jung, Lewis experienced two distinct aspects of himself — an inner, spiritual self and an exterior, worldly self. In his autobiography *Surprised by Joy*, he describes how as a child he experienced moments of awe and a sense of transportation when in nature. There were also a few occasions in his early childhood which evoked in him a profound sense of joy. One was when his older brother brought a toy garden — a biscuit tin filled with moss — into the house: it stirred a longing associated with an 'enormous bliss', and almost as soon as these emotions were felt they were gone, returning him to the commonplace world.[125]

Lewis's early childhood was generally very happy. He enjoyed a rich imagination along with these extra-ordinary moments that spoke of another dimension to life. Interestingly, at the same time as having this capacity for joy, he experienced a series of terrifying dreams: how, he wondered, could protected childhood have within it, 'a window opening on what is hardly less than Hell'?[126] Indeed, being available to the archetypal (transpersonal and transcendent) aspect of joy also means being sensitive to the archetypal intensity of shame and guilt, which take on terrifying symbolic form in our imagination as expressed in dreams. (Jung felt that early childhood [because of the underdeveloped rational mind] was a time in which the psyche was very available to the archetypes.)

Lewis's transcendent experiences of joy ended with the death of his mother and his move to boarding school — both events were a severe blow that moved him squarely into the harsh realities of the external world. Soon, not even the memory or the desire of joy remained. Many years later, however, this memory was to return through his discovery of Wagner's music and Nordic and Celtic myths. Lewis was then boarding at college, which was a generally depressing experience, and the profound happiness he felt listening to Wagner and reading myths introduced a new duality into his life: an inner life of joy and wonder and an outer one that seemed hopeless, dreary and coarse — two lives lived simultaneously, as different as oil and water.

Lewis's No.2 personality had re-emerged but he wasn't yet able to integrate it with his No.1. This situation was to last many years and eventually resolve after Lewis, in his thirties, discovered the writings of Christian mystics. These works gave an intellectual context to the abstract, inner experiences of joy he had obtained through music and myths —the writings of the mystics allowed him to view his experiences of joy within a spiritual context. *The Chronicles of Narnia* (containing Christian and mythological themes) — were a product of this, marrying his childhood fantasies of a place he called 'Animal Land' with his later intellectual understanding of the source of his experiences of joy — a contact with holiness.

The mid-life crisis heralds a rebirth of our No.2 personality and the skills developed in the first half of life can then be used as vehicles for expressing our spiritual nature. Each of us will be attracted to a specific arena that provides us with the richest means of connecting with our Self and sense of inner authority — where we feel the most confident and free. I find it fascinating to observe the change in people as they step into and out of their 'arena'. Singers who exude boldness and strength while performing for example can seem shy and uncertain when interviewed off stage. This is why we often can't imagine ourselves being able to do what someone else does, and vice versa — it's never too difficult to do what our Self calls us to do, but it is inordinately difficult to go against it.

Some people find a perfect fit in terms of their arena early on in life and they stick with it, gradually integrating their No.2 personality into the form of their work as time goes by. For others, there is movement from one field to another as integration progresses, culminating in what is felt to be the most fulfilling arena later in life. The following quote of Nietzsche's (though his concept of power leaves a lot to be desired, he nonetheless had many profound insights) is a wonderful description of how all of our experiences in life can come together under the principle of an 'organising idea'. In Jungian terms this principle is the expression of the wholeness of the personality, and in the Course's terms is the expression of the wholeness of the Self:

> *The organising 'idea,' which is destined to become master, grows and continues to grow into the depths — it begins to command, it leads you slowly back from your deviations and aberrations, it prepares individual qualities and capacities, which one day will make themselves felt as indispensable to the whole of your task — step by step it cultivates all the serviceable faculties, before it ever whispers a word concerning the dominant task, the 'goal,' the 'object,' and the 'meaning' of it all.*[127]

In relation to *A Course in Miracles*, practicing forgiveness is what gradually integrates our No.1 and No.2 personalities, with the fear of spiritual experience lessening as we let go of shame and guilt. And it is this integration — the ultimate 'organising idea' — that also leads us to the most fruitful and rewarding expression of our wholeness in terms of our outer life's work. Moving through the Dark Night often entails discovering and moving with this new focus — it can help to steady our course as we begin the process of ascent and encounter puzzling oscillations between darkness and light.

Great Fluctuations in Mood

Just as the depth of the Dark Night of the Soul is approached gradually (as we notice our spiritual connection to be waning along with our capacity to deal with daily duties and irritants) the process of emerging from the Dark Night is generally slow. One grievance after another seems to lessen its hold on our experience as we practice forgiveness, and our general experience of anxiety and depression ease accordingly. Paradoxically however, the ascent is also marked by pronounced oscillations between strong experiences of love and hate, joy and pain, which can alternate rapidly. It's not uncommon that a day in which we feel we've made progress and let go of something from the past to be followed by one in which we feel worse. In Evelyn Underhill's extensive study of mysticism, she notes this experience as a common thread in the personal accounts of mystics:

> *The typical mystic seems to move towards his goal through a series of strongly marked oscillations between 'states of pleasure' and 'states of pain.' The existence and succession of these states... can be traced, to a greater or lesser degree, in almost every case of which we possess anything like a detailed record... The soul, as it treads the ascending spiral of its road towards reality, experiences alternately the sunshine and the shade. These experiences are 'constants' of the transcendental life.*[128]

The cause of these oscillations is again our resistance: the fear we feel at the thought of losing the self we think we need to survive. The problem, as Underhill phrases it, is that we have 'two thirsts' — for the 'superficial consciousness' of our self, and for our Self:

> *The 'two thirsts' of the superficial and spiritual consciousness assert themselves by turns. Each step towards the vision of the Real brings with it a reaction. The nascent transcendental powers are easily fatigued, and the pendulum of*

> *self takes a shorter swing. 'I was swept up to Thee by Thy Beauty, and torn away from Thee by my own weight,' says St. Augustine.*[129]

The more profound our experience of freedom or joy as we begin to express the wholeness of our Self, the faster and stronger our counter feelings of anger, hurt, fear or depression. We can also become preoccupied with our body — old issues related to how it lets us down in certain respects — because rooting our awareness and identity in the body is another way of protecting our ego identification.

Holding on to anger that comes up is a great temptation as we ascend, and this will hurt us more than before because of the contrast with the joy we have felt. The difference between heaven and hell — now more clearly defined — leads to a more intense sense of loss when we step back into our ego. And yet the temptation is to dig our heels in and remain in our one-sided perspective of people and events long past, even though doing so feels worse than before. We're also likely to project old themes of victimhood onto present circumstances more frequently.

It's important to be vigilant then, for our mind wandering back to grievances and lingering in them. Now is the time for perspective: we need to understand that this oscillation is an inevitable part of the process out of the Dark Night, and that we have indeed made progress despite how we feel. We need to resist the human tendency to focus on the negative and 'pick at it' rather than appreciate the positive growth we've made. Not only does this mean watching out for our negative thoughts, but for our seemingly positive ones too: hopes and fantasies of obtaining recognition through a given notion of success or lingering on the appreciation and flattery of others. These things keep the past alive — when we cling to them, we're trying to make up for a lack of love and support in the past. Craving and loathing, fantasy and fear, are again signs we've identified with our ego and our solutions.

Rather than being a source of discouragement, we can regard our 'great oscillations' as an indicator that we are actually making moves toward our goal, otherwise there would be no throwback into the pain of our ego identification. They are a sign that we are on the threshold of a new state; they are part of 'the effort to establish a new equilibrium, to get, as it were, a firm foothold upon transcendent levels of reality'.[130] With this in mind, when we find ourselves lost in the darkness of a reflexive retreat to our ego it's helpful to acknowledge that we have become afraid of embracing our Self, and not judge ourselves for this.

The early stages of addressing our shame and guilt involve working through the process of forgiveness as described in Chapter Eight. As long as we feel resistance to looking at a particular issue or relationship, then it's perhaps a good sign that we need to look at the specific fears and beliefs surrounding it. We will reach a point, however, where we find that moments of irritation and despair can gradually dissolve by simply viewing our lack of peace as a result of clinging to our ego.

The Return

> *It is easy in the world to live after the world's opinion; it is easy in solitude to live after our own; but the great man is he who in the midst of the crowd keeps with perfect sweetness the independence of solitude.*[131]
>
> Ralph Waldo Emerson

> *Take note of how you are inwardly turned to God... and maintain this same attitude of mind, preserving it when you go among the crowd, into restlessness and diversity.*[132]
>
> Meister Eckhart

During the Dark Night of the Soul we need to retreat from the world to a certain degree in order to experience and cope with the depths of the process. In turn, re-engaging with the world (albeit from a different 'space') is a necessary part of emerging from the Dark Night, as it helps us to truly integrate our experience: it's in our interactions with others that we consolidate our newfound sense of Self. An awareness that we have some experience or expertise that could assist others is often what helps us emerge — it acts as a magnet to help pull us out of the Night. A growing sense of community, therefore, has a rehabilitative effect and inspires us to make the return — where before the world seemed barren, we now feel something positive towards it in recognition of the purpose it can serve as a setting for forgiveness and healing.

A feeling of freedom and new beginnings accompany us as we move forward. The message of the mystics, says Underhill, is that there is much to do; that our life is just beginning:

> *Most people work so hard developing their correspondence with the visible world, that their power of corresponding with the invisible is left in a rudimentary state. But when, for one reason or another, we begin to wake up a little bit, to lift the nose from the ground and notice that spiritual light and that spiritual atmosphere as real constituents of our human world; then, the whole situation is changed. Our horizon is widened, our experience is enormously enriched,*

and at the same time our responsibilities are enlarged.[133]

What makes all of this possible is that we now know — not just intellectually, but experientially — that we're not alone; that Help/Truth/our Self travel with us. We need only make room for them by being willing to question our judgements and open our minds to their influence. This guidance will help us live the life that is ours more completely than ever before and inspire us with an energy that facilitates its expression: when we judge on our own, we starve ourselves of this 'daily bread'. A major boon of the Dark Night therefore is the establishment of a living dialogue with Truth. Nobody can *teach* Truth or Love; it's something that each of us needs to develop a personal relationship with.

The happiness experienced as a result of passing through the Dark Night relates to this awareness that there is a loving guide within us. Though we still have moments of self-doubt they don't have the impact they had before. With a measure of our own wealth, wholeness and eternal safety, we'll also no longer be so disturbed by our own faults or those of others, and things generally won't bother us like they used to. Trusting in our essential goodness, the world will also seem less threatening because we won't expect or fear abandonment and punishment. Saint Teresa of Avila likened this experience to seeing all that goes on around you from a height beyond harm's way. Likewise, *A Course in Miracles* speaks of being lifted up to look on the world from 'the quiet sphere above the battleground' where we gain a perspective that enables us to remain peaceful (T-23.IV.9.5).

From this vantage point we won't experience the compulsiveness or obsessiveness of our solutions, and so we'll also carry a sense of *rest* with us no matter what goes on around us or how busy we are: 'This quiet centre, in which you do nothing, will remain with you, giving you rest in the midst of every busy doing on which you are sent' (T-18.VII.8.3). Whether we serve life in a quiet or dynamic way in form, we'll remain at rest within, acting without the 'shoulds' and 'oughts' of shame and guilt. Trust — in who we are and Who is with us — and transcending the restlessness of not being ourselves, is what makes this possible.

True Autonomy

Asking for Help reflects the beginning of independent thought. The development of trust — in ourselves and our Source; in who we are and what supports us — is what fosters true independence because it gives us the courage and perspective to move beyond the dictates and emotional demands of our solutions. It might seem ironic that moving beyond emotional dependency goes hand-in-hand with appreciating our dependence on Help. However, acknowledging this dependency — for guidance and for the love and sense of security that we long for — is the way out of our strong emotional dependency on others.

Discovering your own voice — your own way — therefore runs parallel to getting in touch with the support of your inner, loving Authority. To be 'authentic' means to let go of an identification with shame and guilt and choose to identify with the wholeness of our Self instead. Likewise, it involves resting in our true character and calling. After all, in the words of the American philosopher Ralph Waldo Emerson, there is no one to 'guard our post' but us.[134] Emerson spoke of the need to be incorruptibly true to our own private conscience, rather than blindly following the dictates and values of others. 'Society everywhere is in conspiracy against the manhood of every one of its members',[135] he wrote. We have a duty to 'see freshly' from our own connection to the divine — Truth, like Beauty, needs to be *experienced* and can't be substituted by the 'dead letter' of a formal, religious canon.

Rules and common values have their place, however routine, habit and tradition can be counterproductive if they prevent us from opening our minds to the guidance of our Self. At some point we have to be willing to turn within for answers, to 'go alone'. The Dark Night of the Soul is the process whereby the courage to be authentic — to truly think for ourselves and act upon our own conscience — is forged. Preceding this, we live much of our life under the influence of other people's perceptions, values, and the demands of our solutions. Self-estrangement eventually leads to the inner crisis of the Dark Night and our process through it establishes a true sense of independence and psychological and spiritual adulthood. It does this by moving us to embody our whole personality and strengthen our faith in our Self at the same time.

Underhill, for example, describes the process of the Dark Night of the Soul as one in which we are 'pressed against our will' to inhabit all aspects of our personality despite our fears:

> *The whole tendency of these trials in the 'path of humanity' seems, as we look at them, to be directed towards the awakening of those elements of character left dormant... We seem to see the 'new man' invading all the resistant or inactive corners of personality: the Servitor of Wisdom being pressed against his will to a deeply and widely human life in the interests of Eternal Love.*[136]

Lessening our identification with our ego doesn't mean we end up a bland version of ourselves, our individual characteristics muted by a growing appreciation of oneness. Socrates, for example, was a fully-fledged individual. His spirituality didn't negate his personality; on the contrary, it helped him to express it. He was able to extend himself to others because he trusted his inherent goodness and so could walk the world with a warmth and unselfconscious energy that said, 'Hello. I am here' — a simple statement of engagement without guilt for existing or the egoism of 'Look at me!' Indeed, by appreciating the guidance of the loving authority within, Socrates was able to be more 'himself' than most others around him; his undeniable presence and uniqueness were the results of a deeply contemplative inner life.

With less inner conflict stemming from shame and guilt we'll also see things more clearly and objectively than before. There will be less tension surrounding yes and no, this way or that way, and we'll be more efficient in our daily tasks as love moves us wholeheartedly in our actions. Our communion with our Self is now at the centre of our lives with childlike dependence and faith that it will lead us where we need to go for the benefit of ourselves and others.

From managing to get by, whether by passively submitting to the impositions of others and life generally, or pushing hard against the world to mould it to our desires, or resigning from meaningful engagement with the world, we emerge from the Dark Night with one common experience: that we're not the self we thought we were, we're not alone and we can trust in the loving authority of our inner Teacher. We now have the foundations for an authentic, living discourse with life — each day, project, and interaction can become for us a new and vital way of expressing our Self, and the means by which we embrace it.

10

The Life of Janet Frame

'Unshakeable is the liberation of my mind', said the Buddha. And as we've seen, Socrates too didn't seem perturbed by much at all. Such spiritual giants light the way and show us what is possible, but they can seem unrelatable to the everyday, 'all-too-human', experience. For this reason, I've decided to conclude this book with a discussion of the life of Janet Frame, one of New Zealand's most celebrated authors. Janet's story illustrates some of the difficulties faced in coming to terms with our autonomy, particularly when our true self seems at odds with the expectations of those around us. It also shows how an appreciation for the transcendent can come in many guises, helping us cope in difficult times and leading to an experience of freedom founded on a connection with our Self — the basis for true emotional autonomy.

Growing Up

Life was very difficult for Janet during the 'first half' of life; but it didn't start out that way. Janet was born in New Zealand, 1926, the third of five children. Her father worked on the railways and her mother was a housemaid, and though they had little money, Janet's early years were happy ones in which she enjoyed playing with her siblings and exploring the surrounding countryside in the coastal town of Oamaru.

The exuberance and fascination of childhood however was soon overshadowed by several experiences that brought the harsh realities of life into focus. The first of these occurred just after Janet started primary school in 1930. She had taken money from her father's trouser pocket and used it to buy chewing gum for her classmates. Her teacher found out but Janet refused to confess that the money was stolen, and thus began a humiliating experience in which she was forced to stand on a platform in front of the entire class for the whole day while they continued their lessons. She felt afraid, friendless, and because she knew her brother and sister would 'tell' as soon as they got home, she never wanted to go home.[137]

When her brother innocently told the teacher that his father hadn't given Janet money, she was found out and confessed. News quickly spread throughout the school that Janet had stolen money from her father, and she was mortified that her future prospects were doomed.[138] Now she had a label that couldn't be shaken off: both at home and school she was called 'thief'.

A few years later, the Frame household was awakened one night by Janet's brother Geordie having a violent convulsion. Geordie was diagnosed with epilepsy and prescribed bromide, which had a stupefying effect on him. Adding to his fear and frustration were merciless taunts at school and his father's insistence that he could stop his seizures 'if he wanted to'. Every day, Geordie flew into fits of rage and threw things around the house and at his siblings, while his father continued to bully him. Apart from the distressing nature of what was going on around her, Janet was also tormented by a sense of guilt: a few nights before Geordie had his first seizure, she had thrown a lump of coal at him and hit him on the head. She then harboured a belief she had caused his epilepsy.[139] Now Janet was not only a 'thief', but she imagined she had damaged her brother as well: her self-concept was well on the way to becoming guilt-prone and this began a preoccupation and worry about the future.

The ramifications of Geordie's illness were far-reaching. Janet's mother focussed her attention on protecting and nursing her son, leaving the other children to fend for themselves. Consequently, Janet often went to school dirty, in ill-fitting clothes and was teased along with her brother, experiencing moments of intense shame. The family finances also took a hit with the cost of Geordie's medications and hospital visits, and Janet's father's wages were cut as the Depression hit its peak. 'The Fall' from Janet's carefree early childhood was now firmly established and had a profound effect on her: she was anxious, had nervous twitches and tics, and was acutely self-conscious. Despite all the turmoil at home, her 'consuming longing' was to be invited to join the skipping games at recess.[140]

There seemed to be nowhere Janet could feel at ease. She was an outcast at primary school and the family home was tumultuous. Then, adding to her despair when she was twelve and preparing to begin her first year at high school, her older sister Myrtle went swimming at the public baths and drowned due to complications from a heart condition. In many ways, Myrtle was Janet's opposite. Myrtle was constantly engaged in battles with her father over boys and parties: she was the 'teasing, pinching, thumping sister', full of life and theatrical ambitions, and yet her life was gone in an instant. The occasion of her sister's death was also the first time Janet saw her father cry.

Janet's time at high school was no less difficult than her experience at primary school, and although she desperately wanted her time there to be over, she didn't feel equipped to take her place in the world. Nonetheless, when she graduated, she was forced to consider what she would *do* in the world. She wanted to be a writer and was clearly talented, but she got the message from those closest to her (and society as a whole) that writing couldn't be considered a serious occupation. Since she did well in her studies and had relatives who'd become teachers, her family assumed she would become a teacher. In keeping with those expectations, Janet left home to board at her aunt's while beginning studies at teachers' college and university.

Desperately aware of all that was unacceptable about her in the eyes of others — her fuzzy red hair, her shyness, her clothes and rotting teeth — Janet set about constructing a repertoire to make herself acceptable. She decided to become the perfect boarder and be as unobtrusive as possible, 'no trouble at all'. To do this she ate very little (frequently going hungry) and spent most of her time in her room. When she was asked to leave her aunt's because she'd eaten her prized chocolates, Janet was tormented by shame, embarrassment, and a sense of loss for no longer being thought of as a 'lovely girl'.[141] Janet had clearly adopted the compliant, self-effacing solution as a way of getting by in the world.

Janet felt an acute sense of difference from those around her during this time and she had no sense of 'place'. After starting university, she felt the identity she had shared with her family was gone. She increasingly saw a pattern of suffering and turmoil in her parents' lives that troubled her and left her feeling helpless, so while she was not without love for them, all her longing was directed towards escaping the fold, quickly and resolutely, so she could leave the pain of home behind.[142] Having stepped out on her own to forge a path for herself Janet felt an increasing distance from her parents, however she didn't feel a part of the world outside of her family. In many ways, Janet was in a constant state of exile.

Crisis

Janet enjoyed her interactions with children during her rounds as a trainee teacher, however she was terrified of being judged on her performance by the superintendent and teachers at the school. She also spent her free time alone instead of in the teachers' lounge because of her shyness and fear of people commenting on her performance. These were significant stresses for Janet. She felt isolated, lost and unhappy pursuing a profession that wasn't really 'her'. She did have some solace in the form of her psychology lecturer at the time, John Money — an attractive man with an appreciation for the arts in general and someone who recognised Janet's significant literary talent.

Money made himself available to Janet for counselling, and they soon conducted regular sessions in which Janet finally found someone who appreciated her desire to be a writer; someone who was sensitive to her need to be understood. She also, however, fell into the compliant type's pattern of seeking refuge and fulfilment in the attention and affection of someone else. Janet was extremely lonely and saw in Money a kindred spirit, someone who perceived and appreciated the depths of who she was. It's little wonder therefore that Janet's attachment to Money soon grew into an obsession: when he happened to smile at her, she was happy for days but when he failed to notice her, she became depressed.[143]

A perfect storm of events led to a crisis point for Janet. Firstly, John Money passed her in the street one day without seeing her.[144] This upset Janet and on the following day her distress was compounded by the advent of the school inspector's crucial teaching assessment. Janet's anxiety got the better of her and as the inspector took his seat at the back of the class Janet walked out of the classroom and the building. At first, she enjoyed a sense of freedom as she left the school behind, but then worries about the future soon took hold. She desperately wanted to break her enrolment but didn't know what else to do. She felt completely isolated and struggled to imagine how she could earn a living in the world and be herself at the same time.

Janet's only sense of relief came from seeing Money at psychology lectures and counselling sessions. To her dismay, however, Money was suddenly replaced with another lecturer, and that weekly resource was gone. Though she still had her sessions with him, it was becoming clear to Money that Janet needed extra help. In consultation with the head of the psychology department, Money felt that the best thing for Janet was to spend some time in hospital and the suggestion appealed to her: there she could have 'a few days' rest', free of the worries of teaching, trying to earn money, her sense of isolation in 'the big wide world', and from being responsible.[145]

After three weeks in hospital, the doctors concluded that there was nothing wrong with Janet, and her mother was contacted to take her home. However, when Mrs Frame arrived and Janet was faced with the prospect of return, she panicked: 'all the worries of the world' returned — the financial stress and 'everlasting toil' of her parents, the arguments at home, and her decaying teeth.[146]

Home was the last place Janet wanted to be. She screamed

at her mother to go away, and to her dismay was subsequently committed as an involuntary patient and moved to Seacliff, a hospital for people with severe mental disturbances. In her autobiography, Janet notes that no one thought to ask her why she had screamed at her mother or what her plans were for the future.[147] Aged twenty-one, these two facets of her life were most relevant to her distress, and — if addressed with sensitivity — might have saved her a great deal of suffering. Instead, Janet became a 'third person' at hospital — spoken about, discussed, but not listened to, and at Seacliff, she was misdiagnosed as having schizophrenia.

Although she met her initial diagnosis with trepidation, Janet also found some comfort in the label 'schizophrenia' as it gave her a concrete means of receiving help. She feared that without her diagnosis, her more 'normal' state of anxiety and stress linked with the common developmental path of wondering how to cope in the world, would draw less attention and practical help than the more 'distinctly signposted path' of schizophrenia. However, Seacliff was anything but a therapeutic environment, and the kind of self-erasure Janet had felt when not consulted about the move to Seacliff was to be a significant feature of her stay there.

Self-Erasure

Janet's hospital admission had the appeal of extricating her from the demands of survival in the outside world, however it came at the cost of her freedom and recognition as an individual. Seacliff functioned like a totalitarian state. The senior staff in charge of writing reports made the majority of the assessments based on how 'co-operative' a patient was, regardless of the reasonableness of the order (to use doorless lavatories, for example), and suggested certain treatments (ECT without anaesthetic, or ice baths) as punishment, under the guise of therapy.[148]

The doctors at Seacliff weren't interested in the Freudian notion of a talking cure: they weren't interested in their patients as people. The patients at Seacliff were involuntary patients, having no legal recognition to make their own decisions, and the doctors treated them accordingly: as non-entities. As with any totalitarian state, independent thought and action was heavily policed and actively discouraged. A sign of health was to 'be good', which meant to be compliant, submissive, to blend into the walls. Janet had been removed from the frying pan, only to find herself in the fire.

About two months after her admission to Seacliff, Janet was released into her family's care. The volatile dynamic between her father and brother was still in full force and the household was tense, so Janet got a live-in position as housemaid, waitress and nurse at a guest house with six boarders and four elderly women. Janet easily stepped into the role of selflessly attending to the needs of others and enjoyed waiting on them. She reflected that she seemed to have been a 'born servant', however the fact that she enjoyed her role so much frightened her: she saw in her enjoyment a desire to erase herself and 'live only through the feelings of others', as she realised her mother had done.[149] This was Janet's dilemma at that point in her life. She could manage the outside world in the role of a compliant type, a servant to others, a shadow in the background, however she was also aware of a strong need to express herself through writing and to establish a career with it.

Janet wrote several short stories while she was out of hospital and continued her sessions with Money, who was keen to read some of her work. Fearing the judgement of others, Janet was reluctant to let him see her work, but agreed in the end. Money was impressed with what he read and offered to submit Janet's stories to a publisher on her behalf. Over the next nine months Janet produced a collection of stories that was later to be her first published book, *The Lagoon*. In the meantime, Janet was again to return to hospital of her own volition because of her distress in the outside world.

What Janet desperately wanted was a place where she could truly rest to gather herself. However, there was nowhere she could call home. The following eight years consisted of extended periods in hospital followed by probations which she welcomed until she'd spent some time at the family home or in cheap boarding houses which were distressing in their own right. After a few weeks she'd return to hospital because there was nowhere else for her to live; yet she was always fearful, 'like a condemned person returning to the executioner'.[150] Janet also longed for a place where she felt she belonged, but her shyness and people's lack of tact always reinforced her sense of alienation. Unfortunately, the closest Janet came to a semblance of 'home' and refuge was in hospital, where at least she was 'believed to be "at home"'.[151]

Lifelines

The years that followed were dominated by unhappiness and fear, and yet Janet survived, her sanity and self intact. Several things contributed to her endurance. Firstly, though she was terrified of the matrons and doctors, she had a real fondness, empathy and even 'parental concern' for her fellow patients. It's ironic that Janet's removal from the regular world and into the confines of hospital enabled her to finally feel a connection with the majority of people around her. She wasn't psychotic, schizophrenic or delusional but she could appreciate the loneliness, sense of difference and lack of place that the other patients suffered from.

Janet was determined to give the people around her a voice, which she did years later in her book *Faces in the Water*: it was her desire to tell their story that enabled her to survive.[152] The motivation to refuse self-erasure (the seductive call of the compliant solution) came from wanting to use her voice to help those who couldn't use their own. I don't believe this desire to help was of a self-effacing nature on Janet's part, but a truly loving motivation based on empathy and a wish to shed light on practices and attitudes that were inhumane. Whether we've been in the habit of using our voice to dominate others, or been scared of using it at all, the pull that helps us out of the Dark Night is to use our voice in loving service of others.

Janet also gained consolation from her copy of Shakespeare's works. Literature was a source of profound beauty and comfort for Janet: it gave her a sense of freedom that transcended her surroundings and spoke of the eternal. To her, acknowledging a great work of art was like 'a flight in paradise'.[153] Connecting to Absolute Beauty as expressed through literature connected Janet with her Self — what she described as a felt connection with an 'inviolable core' from which she drew strength amongst the squalor and inhumanity of her environment.[154]

Her copy of Shakespeare was confiscated on several occasions because the powers-that-be didn't think an interest in literature was a healthy preoccupation for the mentally unwell, but when Janet's schemes to have it returned were successful, she clung to it as a friend. Janet also enjoyed the occasional visit from friends who appreciated her writing ambition and with whom she could share conversation about writing, authors and books. One friend gave her a small photograph of writer Henry James's house in Sussex — another object along with her copy of Shakespeare that reminded her of who she was, her vocation, and the value of her poetic imagination which her doctors regarded as problematic.

Accompanying Janet's sense of her Self — or 'No.2 personality' — was a belief that something else transcendent was available to her for support and assistance. Janet's mother Lottie was a Christadelphian and the Bible was one of few books in the house — consequently it was pored over by the Frame children as a source of wondrous stories and adventures. Lottie would also read it to them on Sundays with the intention of furthering their faith in God's providence and love.

Janet wasn't a religious person in the usual sense, nor did she wish to belong to another institution, however one night, trying to sleep with sores and a discharging ear amid the squalor and cries of distress from patients in the ward she shared, she touched on the possibility of totally losing her identity to the world of insanity around her, and in her terror recited Psalm 23:

> *The Lord is my shepherd... though I walk through the valley of the shadow of death, I will fear no evil; for Thou art with me; Thy rod and Thy staff, they comfort me.*

In his biography of Janet, Michael King describes how just saying the words of the Psalm was a comfort to her, and the next morning Janet was moved back to a ward she remembered as 'an oasis', taking this as a sign that calls for Help *are* answered and that something was looking after her — a conviction she retained for the rest of her life.[155]

Two more significant events added to the salvific affect of being moved back to the 'oasis': shortly after arriving, Janet received a parcel containing a published copy of her book *The Lagoon*; and the hospital's superintendent was replaced with someone who had an appreciation for literature. Upon seeing Janet's book, he decided that writing wasn't a negative influence on her mental health and allowed her access to her typewriter in hospital. Just as a 'perfect storm' of events had led to Janet's admission to hospital and her depths of despair, a series of synchronous, 'positive' events helped to lead her out of it.

It's noteworthy that Janet's prayer for help was met with confirmation: that she wasn't alone, help was available, and her writing ambitions were valid. At the lowest point of her life, Janet's prayer from the depths of her being reflected a decision to go on, to not succumb to self-erasure and to fulfil her destiny by embodying the wholeness of her personality and her Self. It's no coincidence that this decisive moment was met with things that consolidated her belief in support from something of a transcendent nature, along with guidance as to the path (writing) that would best express her Self: these things are inextricably linked.

A nadir ('rock-bottom') experience often comes at a fork in the road where we need to decide whether we want to continue living our lives to try and fulfil the defensive needs of our solution (to be 'good' or 'successful' for example), or to find another way. The declaration that there *must* be a better way expresses a call for Help, which is also the call to our Self. This 'Road to Damascus' moment in which we choose another purpose for our lives, is a moment of conversion in which faith in our solutions is converted to faith in the process and promise of healing.

The answers to Janet's prayer were cases of synchronicity — the meaningful coincidences that help guide us on our path and reassure us of the value of marching on. Indeed, just like Janet Frame, we are all assisted in the task of integrating our inner and outer worlds — our spiritual Self and the way we can best give it form in the world — as we make ourselves available to Help. In Jungian terms, our willingness to face the task of embodying our Self prepares the ground for a 'compensatory reaction from the collective unconscious',[156] which is Jung's way of saying that our availability to Help will always be met with a response from the wisdom of our Self, and this will be reflected in some form of guidance: a dream, an inclination to take more notice of our intuition (to *listen*), moments of synchronicity.

And as we are helped to emerge from a profound darkness, we bring with us a unique perspective that couldn't have been gained any other way. It's when we find out what supports us when we can no longer support ourselves that we begin to tap into the joy buried beneath our despair. As we touch upon the archetypal nature and intensity of our shame and guilt, we slowly approach our Self and a joy of equally archetypal proportions. As the French mystic Madame Guyon wrote, a 'seed of immortality' is laid amongst our complete despair.[157]

The Envoy

The act of writing itself was a major lifeline for Janet. It was her bridge between the spiritual aspects of her No.2 personality and her No.1 personality — the latter had to navigate the world and its terms. The death of her sister Myrtle was the catalyst for a profound shift in Janet's relationship to her imagination. In the aftermath of the tragedy, Janet had explored the book of poetry, *Mount Helicon,* which was part of the curriculum for secondary school, and discovered that what many of the poets wrote suggested they knew exactly how Janet felt, and of the tragedy of Myrtle's death.[158]

The poets conveyed a depth of understanding of Janet's experience despite their distance in time and space. This was something of a revelation for Janet. In the past, she had been interested in both reading and composing adventures — the products of a 'fanciful' imagination. Now, in reading *Mount Helicon* she saw that a 'poetic' imagination could shed light on universal, shared experiences involving the everyday triumphs and tragedies of life, and so help to inform and thus *transform* our relationship to them. She wanted to use her imagination to shine a light on the 'world of fact', not to force her 'to exist in an "elsewhere"'.[159]

Janet's engagement with her poetic imagination through writing was how she could integrate her inner, spiritual reality with her external world. Janet's writing wasn't a means of escaping her difficult circumstances by constructing fantasies — it was a way in which she connected with the transcendent aspect of herself and expressed that connection in the world. Her poetic imagination enabled her to reflect on the goings on around her from a perspective that saw common, universal themes being acted out, and in this sense, it was 'religious'. Indeed, from a very early age Janet had an inclination for tapping into the existential 'big picture' elements underlying our experience: in her autobiography she describes a time when she was seven, looking down an empty dusty road, 'listening to the wind and its sad song', and knew this 'outside sadness' belonged, not to herself, but to the world.[160]

The decision Janet made after Myrtle died, to develop her poetic imagination instead of indulge her fanciful imagination, was a decision to use her writing to touch the world around her from the perspective of transcendent truths from above. This manifested in an extraordinary ability to understand the depths of the human experience and write about it with clarity. Janet later called her poetic imagination The Envoy. It was her 'watching self', which transported the seemingly mundane experiences of everyday life to 'Mirror City' — her imagination, where the facts and circumstances of life mirrored common mythic, archetypal themes, thereby imbuing them with meaning. In other words, personal experiences, challenges and problems carry mythic themes: the arrival; departure; marriage; death. To see the mythic in the ordinary is the gift of a poetic imagination, and for Janet The Envoy was an ever-present resource, a lifeline.

The ability to perceive the goings on of the world as symbolically reflecting universal themes is beneficial for two main reasons. Janet recognised that the underlying fabric of life runs according to well-worn narratives *that we all share*. She therefore had an appreciation for our common ground, needs and challenges, and this would have mitigated her sense of personal and existential loneliness.

Moreover, awareness of our *shared* conflicts, needs and struggles moves us toward an appreciation of Oneness and our eternal Self — Janet's 'inviolable core' — availing us of a transcendent source of peace. All of this helps to locate us 'above the battleground', a step removed from the limitations and chaos of the world around us because we can look at it from a different perspective. Indeed, Janet referred to language as 'the hawk suspended above eternity' — it was that which gave her a sense of connection to the transcendent and which informed her perceptions of the world.[161]

Janet's writing also saved her in a very literal sense. During her later years in hospital she was put on a list for a leucotomy

— a radical (now obsolete) treatment for schizophrenia in which neural tracts in the frontal lobes of the brain are severed. She was told that the operation would be good for her and would hasten the time of her release from hospital, but Janet felt that this would ensure her final erasure. She recalled the ward nurse's description of another patient who had had the procedure with 'outstanding results': the patient now sold hats in a shop. Wouldn't Janet prefer to be without her fancy writing aspirations and be content with doing something ordinary, something normal, like selling hats in a shop?[162]

Nearing the day of surgery, Janet was visited by the superintendent of the hospital who said he was taking her off the list. A daily newspaper had announced that Janet was the winner of a prestigious writing award for *The Lagoon*.

Freedom

Not long after she won the award, arrangements were made for Janet's release from hospital. She was twenty-nine years old and looked forward to returning home, despite its problems, because of the appeal of freedom. Where in the past she was fearful of making decisions and of the future, Janet left hospital feeling energised at the thought of being able to execute her own authority. She could decide what she wanted to do, where she wanted to go, and she could acknowledge the validity of her feelings and aspirations for her future — thus, words that used to inspire fear, 'decide' and 'future', now took on a brighter hue.[163]

Janet had experienced the depths of 'nothingness' in hospital, having been forced into a constant state of compliance and docility. Her nadir was one in which she felt the threat of total self-erasure, but also the moment where she said no to disappearing. The horror of touching on the extreme conclusion of a compliant solution — no self — shocked her into looking forward to, rather than dreading, the idea of her own autonomy. Being able to make decisions and be an active agent in her own future was now experienced as liberating rather than daunting.

Janet stayed briefly at home until she found alternative accommodation. She felt an expectation on the part of her parents that she would stay home and look after them — what else, after all, would she want to do if she wasn't married or a teacher? But since the appeal of self-erasure had gone for Janet, she decided not to postpone her future any longer and moved into an army hut on the property of another New Zealand author, Frank Sargeon. At Sargeon's, Janet developed a daily writing routine and began to find her feet as an author. Eventually, with the assistance of a government grant, she headed for London to pursue her writing career.

Apart from the benefit of a well-connected and supportive writing community, London was home to one of the most progressive and well-regarded psychiatric hospitals in the world. There, at Maudsley hospital, Janet was able to access the counselling services as an outpatient, and found the treatment services and philosophy to be significantly more enlightened than what she had experienced in New Zealand. The psychiatrists listened to their patients and were kind. Janet felt recognised, acknowledged and cared about, and she was grateful for the contrast.

Even as Janet's career began to take shape, she experienced significant bouts of anxiety and depression, so the Maudsley was a blessing. Her doctors helped Janet unearth herself and deal with the trauma of her past. They also helped her address the fact that she was often surrounded by people who decided they knew what was good for her and would take it upon themselves to plan her future. Because Janet's habitual, reflexive response was to play a submissive role, part of her therapy involved learning that she was an adult who could make her own decisions: she recognised that she had been in the role of victim as people around her took it upon themselves to tell her what she should like and do. For much of her life, she'd been a target of the 'You should-ers', but it was time to begin afresh.[164]

Janet could see how she was like her mother in her desire to appear good, her lack of assertiveness and her recourse to poetry when she felt low. She hated her mother's self-effacing 'unselfishness' and her habit of citing scripture or singing hymns to suppress her anger. Having adopted an extreme form of the compliant solution herself, Janet couldn't tolerate seeing its reflection in her mother, nor it's opposite in her father.

It took Janet many years to work through the ingrained habits of the compliant solution. As is often the case with compliant types, each time Janet achieved some success she would grind to a halt. She'd become fatigued, stop writing and be filled with doubt when a book was accepted for publication. Perhaps she didn't want to publish after all, she'd reason. Or if she did publish, maybe she'd prefer just a few copies for friends. At these times, feelings of nothingness would return, an indication that Janet still feared her own success and self-expression and so felt the need to retreat into nothingness as a form of self-sabotage.

Nonetheless, these periods of retreat did not ultimately get the better of Janet. She kept moving on step by step with the aid of her doctors, friends and writing, and managed to do all that was required to further her career. She dealt with agents, publishers and government agencies, and travelled overseas. The help of one doctor in particular, Dr Cawley, was central to the awakening of Janet's own sense of authority. In uncovering and embracing her true nature, Janet was able to do what *she* wanted and valued without shame or guilt. She was able to let go of her solution and embrace who she was.

With her growing self-acceptance, Janet was able to deflect the judgements of others and have the fortitude to assume her life-long ambition to be a full-time writer. Her doctor reminded her that she could live as she wished and not as others thought she should, and that she had no obligations to 'mix'. She did go against Dr Cawley's advice however in deciding to return to New Zealand upon the death of her father, her mother having died a few years earlier. Janet's brother had written to her of her father's death and the need to organise the family's belongings, and she said she would help.

Returning to New Zealand, Janet wasn't the vulnerable person that had left. As Janet integrated the positive aspects of her nature, her perspective of her past was less bound up with resentment and grief and she could revive some pleasant memories from it. When she was leaving London for example, she wasn't occupied with thoughts of the wonders of London she was leaving behind — the buildings, galleries and world of contemporary literature — but of sharing moments with her father as they read cheap, poorly written detective stories. In other words, Janet had forgiven her father. A key part of this healing involved establishing her career as a writer and being able to tap into her 'place' within, a place 'at a deeper level than any landscape of any country would provide'.[165]

By the time Janet returned to New Zealand, she'd made peace between her inner and outer worlds. In the outer, she could indeed make a living from being a writer — it was as legitimate an occupation as anything else — and through her writing she could express the wealth of her spiritual Self. Near the conclusion of Janet's autobiography, we get the sense of a person finding their inner strength and true authority as they shed the shackles of self-doubt. After reading mixed reviews for one of her published works, Janet reflects on the impossibility of pleasing everybody and the foolishness of trying to do so. She affirms that as a writer she must be prepared to stand by her own decisions and choices and maintain her own judgement, however imperfect they might turn out to be. It no longer matters to Janet whether she is right or wrong, but that she trusts and accepts herself. This self-respect becomes her foundation.

Janet never claimed to be enlightened, however I think it's safe to say that she experienced life beyond the 'common unhappiness' prevalent in the world. Indeed, film director Jane Campion was struck by Frame's humour, happiness, energy and aura of freedom when they met to discuss making a film based on Janet's autobiography.[166] The process of stepping into our authority involves trust: a belief that acting on what we feel to be right from the core of our Self will take us wherever we need to be and provide us with all that we need to keep going. Janet's life shows that those who engage in the task of integration emerge with a creative output — in whatever form it takes — that becomes a profound gift to themselves and others.

Bibliography

A Course in Miracles, 1996, 2nd edition, Viking/Penguin Books, U.S.A.

Abersole, PD, *Hit so Hard: The Life and Near Death Story of Patty Schemel*, Shock, 2012. DVD.

Adler, A 1998, *Understanding Human Nature*, Hazelden Foundation, U.S.A.

Alexander, F 1961, 'Remarks about the Relation of Inferiority Feelings to Guilt Feelings', in AS Watson (ed.), *The Scope of Psychoanalysis: Selected Papers of Franz Alexander*, Basic Books Inc., New York.

Aurelius, M, *The Meditations of Marcus Aurelius*, trans. G Long, Kindle Edition.

Becker, E 1997, *The Denial of Death*, Free Press Paperbacks, New York.

Branson, R 2017, *Finding my Virginity: The New Autobiography*, Portfolio-Penguin Books, U.S.A.

Britton, R 1991, 'The Oedipus Situation and the Depressive Position', in R Anderson (ed.), *Clinical Lectures on Klein and Bion*, Routledge, UK.

Bronte, E 2007, 'Stanzas', in J Black, L Conolly, K Flint, I Grundy, D LePan, R Liuzza, JJ McGann, AL Prescott, BV Qualls & C Waters (eds.), *Broadview Anthology of British Literature*, Broadview Press, London.

Butler, D.S & Moseley, L 2003, *Explain Pain*, Noigroup Publications, Adelaide, Australia.

Campbell, J 2011, *A Joseph Campbell Companion: Reflections on the Art of Living*, Joseph Campbell Foundation, Kindle Edition.

Campbell, J 1993, *The Hero with a Thousand Faces*, Fontana Press, London.

Carnegie, D 2001, *How to Win Friends and Influence People*, Harper Collins, Australia.

Davis, WS 2004, *Readings in Ancient History: Greece and the East*, University Press of the Pacific, U.S.A.

Dickson-Wright, C 2007, *Spilling the Beans*, Hodder & Stoughton, U.K.

Dostoevsky, F 2013, *Notes from Underground*, Dead Dodo Vintage, Kindle Edition.

Doyle, AC 2012, *The Complete Sherlock Holmes: with an Introduction from Robert Ryan*, Simon & Schuster U.K., Kindle Edition.

Emerson, RW 1907, *Essays*, Merrill Co., New York, Kindle Edition.

Emerson, RW 2012, *Self-Reliance and Other Essays*, Dover, U.S.A.

Emerson, RW 1969, *The Journals and Miscellaneous Notebooks of Ralph Waldo Emerson,* Vol 7:1838-1842, AW Plumstead & H Hayford (eds.), The Belknap Press of Harvard University Press, U.S.A.

Fine, C 2010, *Delusions of gender: the real science behind sex differences*, Icon Books Ltd., London.

Frame, J 2008, *An Angel at my Table*, Random House Australia, Kindle Edition.

Frame, J 1982, *Faces in the Water*, George Braziller, Inc., U.S.A.

Frame, J 2008, *Living in the Maniototo*, Vintage Books, Australia.

Freud S 2011, *Beyond the Pleasure Principle*, Vook Inc., Kindle

Edition.

Freud, S 2013, *Civilization and its Discontents*, Kindle Edition.

Freud, S 1995, 'Family Romances', in P Gay (ed.), *The Freud Reader*, Vintage Books, London.

Freud, S 2013, *Inhibitions, Symptoms and Anxiety*, Read Books Ltd., Kindle Edition.

Freud, S 2001, 'Some Character-Types Met with in Psychoanalytic Work', in J Strachey (ed.), *The Standard Edition of the Complete Psychological Works of Sigmund Freud*, Vol. 14, The Hogarth Press, London.

Freud, S 1995, 'Wild Psychoanalysis', in P Gay (ed.), *The Freud Reader*, Vintage Books, London.

Frey-Rohn, L 1990, *From Freud to Jung: A Comparative Study of the Psychology of the Unconscious*, Shambala, Boston, MA.

Fromm-Reichmann, F 1959, 'Loneliness', *Psychiatry: Interpersonal and Biological Processes*, 22(1).

Gelman, M et al 2000, 'Viktor Emil Frankl 1905–1997', *American Journal of Psychiatry*, 157(4).

Gordon, B 2017, *Bryony Gordon's Mad World: Prince Harry*, podcast, The Telegraph, 16 April.

Green, H 1978, *I Never Promised you a Rose Garden*, Pan Books Ltd., London.

Guyon, J 1875, *Spiritual Torrents*, Trans. AW Marston, Marston, Low & Searle, London, Kindle Edition.

Hinshelwood, R.D 1994, *Clinical Klein*, Free Association Books, London.

Horney, K 1999, *Neurosis and Human Growth: The Struggle Toward Self-Realisation* , Routledge, London.

Horney, K 1942, *The Collected Works of Karen Horney*, Vols. 1 and 2, WW Norton & Company, New York.

Hughes, B 2011, *The Hemlock Cup: Socrates, Athens and the*

Search for the Good Life, Vintage, London.

Huguelet P, Perroud N 2005, 'Wolfgang Amadeus Mozart's Psychopathology in Light of the Current Conceptualization of Psychiatric Disorders', Psychiatry, 68(2).

Jeremias, J 1966, *Rediscovering the Parables*, SCM Press, London.

Johnson, P 2013, *Mozart*, Viking, New York.

Johnston, C 2015, 'Inside the Mind of a Whimpering, Weeping Killer', *The Age*, 27 March.

Johnston, DC 2017, *The Making of Donald Trump*, Melville House, U.S.A.

Joinson, C 1992, 'Coping with Compassion Fatigue', *Nursing*, 22(4).

Joyce, J 1982, *A Portrait of the Artist as a Young Man*, Granada, London.

Jung, C. G. 2008, C.G. *Jung on Nature, Technology and Modern Life*, M Sabini (ed.), North Atlantic Books, U.S.A.

Jung, C.G. 1989, *Memories, Dreams, Reflections*, Vintage Books, U.S.A.

Jung, C.G. 2004, *Modern Man in Search of a Soul*, Routledge Classics, London.

Jung, C. G. 1978, *Psychological Reflections: A New Anthology of his Writings 1905–1961*, J Jacobi & RFC Hull (eds.), Princeton University Press, New York.

Jung, C.G. 1990, *The Archetypes and the Collective Unconscious*, Princeton University Press, U.S.A.

Kafka, F 2008, *Dearest Father*, Oneworld Classics, U.K.

Kafka, F 2006, *The Judgement*, Penguin Books, London.

Kaler, SR & Freeman, BJ 1994, 'Analysis of Environmental Deprivation: Cognitive and Social Development in Romanian Orphans', *Journal of Child Psychiatry*, 35(4).

Kets DeVries, MFR 1996, 'The Anatomy of the Entrepreneur:

Clinical Observations', *Human Relations*, 49(7).

King, M 2000, *Wrestling with the Angel: A Life of Janet Frame*, Picador, Sydney.

Klein, M 1997, *Envy and Gratitude and other Works 1946-1963*, Vintage, Great Britain.

Lawrence, C 2001, *Swooning: A Classical Music Guide to Life, Love, Lust and Other Follies*, Knopf, Sydney.

Lewis, CS 2002, *Surprised by Joy*, Harper Collins Publishers, London.

Lewis, HB 1987, 'Shame and the Narcissistic Personality', in DL Nathanson (ed.), *The Many Faces of Shame*, The Guilford Press.

Lundin, RW 2015, *Alfred Adler's Basic Concepts and Implications*, Routledge, U.S.A.

Luquet, GH et al., eds., *New Larousse Encyclopedia of Mythology*, Crescent Book, New York, 1987.

Maslow, AH 1993, *The Farther Reaches of Human Nature*, Penguin Books, New York.

Mathieu, F 2007, 'Running on Empty: Compassion Fatigue in Health Professionals', *Rehab & Community Care Medicine*, Spring edition.

May, R 1977, *The Meaning of Anxiety*, Washington Square Press, New York.

Meister Eckhart 1994, *Selected Writings*, Penguin Classics, U.K.

Meyer, JE & Meyer R 1987, 'Self-Portrayal by a Depressed Poet: A Contribution to the Clinical Biography of William Cowper', *The American Journal of Psychiatry*, 144(2).

Mold, A 2013, 'Repositioning the Patient: Patient Organizations, Consumerism, and Autonomy in Britain during the 1960s and 1970s', *Bulletin of the History of Medicine*, Summer edition.

Mother Teresa 1995, *A Simple Path*, Rider, London.

Murray, J. A. C. 1938, *An Introduction to Christian Psychotherapy*,

T&T Clark, Edinburgh.

Nietzsche, F 2017, *Ecce Homo: How One Becomes What One is*, Translated by AM. Ludovici, LRP, Kindle Edition.

O'Connor, P 1990, *Understanding Jung*, Mandarin, Melbourne.

Orwell, G 2004, *Why I Write*, Penguin Books Australia, Ringwood, Victoria.

Oster, E 2004, 'Witchcraft, Weather and Economic Growth in Renaissance Europe', *Journal of Economic Perspectives*, 18(1).Pascal, B 2008, *Human Happiness*, Penguin Books, London.

Pascal, B 2015, 'Pensées', in L Tolstoy (ed.), *A Calendar of Wisdom*, Alma Classics, U.K.

Piers, G & Singer, MB 1971, *Shame and Guilt: A Psychoanalytic and a Cultural Study,* WW Norton, New York.

Plato 2009, *The Collected Dialogues*, E Hamilton & H Cairns (eds.), Princeton University Press, New Jersey.

Ramakrishna 2011, *The Original Gospel of Ramakrishna* , World Wisdom Books, Indiana, USA.

Rosselli, J 1998, *The Life of Mozart*, Cambridge University Press, UK.

Sacks, O 2015, 'My Own Life', *The New York Times.*

Sacks, O 2007, *Musicophilia: Tales of Music and the Brai*n, Picador, UK.

Saint John of the Cross 2003, *The Dark Night of the Soul*, Dover Publications, Kindle Edition.

Salinger, JD 1991, *Franny and Zooey,* Little, Brown and Company, Boston.

Satten, J et. al., 1960, 'Murder Without Apparent Motive: A Study in Personality Disorganisation', *American Journal of Psychiatry*, July Edition, pp. 48-53.

Schemel, P 2017, *Hit so Hard: A Memoir*, Da Capo Press, New York.

Sembou, E 2003, 'Hegel's Idea of a "Struggle for Recognition": The "Phenomenology of Spirit"', *History of Political Thought,* 24(2), pp. 262-281.

Seneca, LA 2011, *Letters from a Stoic*, Seedbox Press, Kindle Edition.

Shelley, M 1988, *Frankenstein*, Oxford University Press, New York.

Singer, J 1994, *Boundaries of the Soul: The Practice of Jung's Psychology*, Prism Press, U.K.

Smart, N 1979, *The Religious Experience of Mankind*, Fount Paperbacks, UK.

Smith, A.P 2008, *The Gnostics: History, Tradition, Scriptures, Influence*, Watkins Publishing, London.

Solomon M 1995, *Mozart: A Life*, HarperCollins Publishers, New York.

Solomon, M 2012, *Beethoven*, Schirmer Trade, London.

Swafford, J 2014, *Beethoven: Anguish and Triumph*, Faber & Faber, London.

Tacey, D 2011, 'Spirituality Individuation and Popular Spirituality', in A Lowe (ed.), *Jung Talks: 50 Years of the C.G. Jung Society of Melbourne*, C.G. Jung Society of Melbourne, Victoria.

Tangney, JP & Dearing, RL 2004, *Shame and Guilt*, The Guilford Press, New York.

Ten-Boom, C 2009, *The Hiding Place*, Baker Publishing Group, Kindle Edition.

Thayer, AW 2016, *The Life of Ludwig van Beethoven*, CreateSpace Independent Publishing Platform, USA.

The Oxford Dictionary of Quotations, 2001, E Knowles (ed.), Oxford University Press, New York.

Tolstoy, L 2005, *A Confession*, Dover Books, U.S.A.

Trump, D 2008, *Think Big*, Harper Business, New York.

Underhill, E 1930, *Mysticism: A Study in Nature and Development of Spiritual Consciousness* , Kindle Edition.

Underhill, E 1914, *Practical Mysticism*, Waxkeep Publishing, Kindle Edition.

Underhill, E 213, *The Spiritual Life*, Martino Fine Books, Kindle Edition.

Waisberg, JL & Page, S 1988, 'Gender Role Nonconformity and Perception of Mental Illness', *Women & Health*, 14(1).

Wapnick, K 1972, 'Mysticism and Schizophrenia', in J White (ed.), *The Highest States of Consciousness* , Doubleday, U.S.A.

Wapnick, K 1994, *Forgiveness and Jesus: The Meeting Place of* A Course in Miracles *and Christianity*, Foundation for *A Course in Miracles*, CA.

Wapnick, K 1990, *Love does not Condemn: The World, the Flesh, and the Devil According to Platonism, Christianity, Gnosticism, and* A Course in Miracles, Foundation for *A Course in Miracles,* New York.

Wehr, G 1988, *Jung: A Biography*, Shambala, Boston, MA.

Notes

PREFACE

1 *A Course in Miracles* doesn't make a clear distinction between shame and guilt, though it refers to both. This is because it uses the word 'guilt' as an umbrella term. For instance, it encapsulates feelings such as inferiority, which are generally associated with shame.

GUILT

2 Kafka, F 2006, *The Judgement*, Penguin Books, London, p. 93.

3 ibid.

4 Kafka, F 2008, *Dearest Father*, Oneworld Classics, U.K., p. 20.

5 ibid., p. 21.

6 Horney, K 1999, *Neurosis and Human Growth: The Struggle Toward Self-Realisation*, Routledge, London, p. 89.

7 Joinson, C 1992, 'Coping with Compassion Fatigue', *Nursing*, 22(4), pp. 16–122.

8 Mathieu, F 2007, 'Running on Empty: Compassion Fatigue in Health Professionals', *Rehab & Community Care Medicine*, Spring edition, p. 2.

9 Gordon, B 2017, *Bryony Gordon's Mad World: Prince Harry*, podcast, The Telegraph, 16 April.

10 Freud, S 2013, *Inhibitions, Symptoms and Anxiety*, Read Books Ltd., Kindle Edition, locations 99–102.

11 Freud, S 2001, 'Some Character-Types Met with in Psychoanalytic Work', in J Strachey (ed.), *The Standard Edition of the Complete Psychological Works of Sigmund Freud*, Vol. 14, The Hogarth Press, London, p. 317.

12 ibid.

13 Huguelet P, Perroud N 2005, 'Wolfgang Amadeus Mozart's Psychopathology in Light of the Current Conceptualization of Psychiatric Disorders', *Psychiatry*, 68(2), pp. 130–9.

14 Horney, K 1942, 'Neurotic Disturbances at Work', *The Collected Works of Karen Horney*, Vol. 2, WW Norton & Company, New York, p. 318.

SHAME

15 Freud, S 1995, 'Family Romances', in P Gay (ed.), *The Freud Reader*, Vintage Books, London, p. 298.

16 Kaler, SR & Freeman, BJ 1994, 'Analysis of Environmental Deprivation: Cognitive and Social Development in Romanian Orphans', *Journal of Child Psychiatry*, 35(4), pp. 769-781.

17 Lewis, HB 1987, 'Shame and the Narcissistic Personality', in DL Nathanson (ed.), *The Many Faces of Shame*, The Guilford Press, p. 99.

18 Johnston, C 2015, 'Inside the Mind of a Whimpering, Weeping Killer', *The Age*, 27 March, pp. 6–7.

19 Horney, K 1942, 'The Expansive Solutions: The Appeal of Mastery', *The Collected Works of Karen Horney*, Vol. 2, WW Norton & Company, New York, pp. 195-196.

20 Kets DeVries, MFR 1996, 'The Anatomy of the Entrepreneur: Clinical Observations', *Human Relations*, 49(7), pp. 853–883.

21 ibid.

22 ibid.

23 ibid.

24 Thayer, AW 2016, *The Life of Ludwig van Beethoven*, CreateSpace Independent Publishing Platform, USA, p. 75.

25 Solomon, M 2012, *Beethoven*, Schirmer Trade, London, p. 371.

26 ibid.

27 Horney, K 1942, 'The Expansive Solutions: The Appeal of Mastery', *The Collected Works of Karen Horney*, Vol. 2, p. 203.

28 Trump, D 2008, *Think Big*, Harper Business, New York, p. 183.

29 Branson, R 2017, *Finding my Virginity: The New Autobiography*, Portfolio-Penguin Books, U.S.A, p. 102.

30 Johnston, DC 2017, *The Making of Donald Trump*, Melville House, U.S.A, p. [illegible].

31 ibid., p. 17.

32 Horney, K 1942, 'The Expansive Solutions: The Appeal of Mastery', *The Collected Works of Karen Horney*, Vol. 2, p. 305.

33 Schemel, P 2017, *Hit So Hard: A Memoir*, Da Capo Press, New York, p. 262.

34 ibid., p. 8.

35 ibid., p. 269.

36 ibid., p. 269.

37 Tangney, JP & Dearing, RL 2004, *Shame and Guilt*, The Guilford Press, New York.

38 ibid.

AVOIDING SHAME AND GUILT

39 Dostoevsky, F 2013, *Notes from Underground*, Dead Dodo Vintage, Kindle Edition, location 389.

40 Doyle, AC 2012, *The Complete Sherlock Holmes: with an Introduction from Robert Ryan*, Simon & Schuster U.K., Kindle Edition, location 25851.

41 Dostoevsky, F 2013, *Notes from Underground*, location 223.

42 Bronte, E 2007, 'Stanzas', in J Black, L Conolly, K Flint, I Grundy, D LePan, R Liuzza, JJ McGann, AL Prescott, BV Qualls & C Waters (eds.), *Broadview Anthology of British Literature*, Broadview Press, London, p. 750.

43 Dostoevsky, F 2013, *Notes from Underground*, location 265.

44 Klein, M 1997, *Envy and Gratitude and other Works 1946–1963*, Vintage, London, pp. 301–302.

45 Fromm-Reichmann, F 1959, 'Loneliness', *Psychiatry: Interpersonal and Biological Processes*, 22(1), p. 1.

46 Green, H 1978, *I Never Promised you a Rose Garden*, Pan Books Ltd., London, p. 227.

47 ibid., p. 139.

RECLAIMING THE SELF

48 Pascal, B 2015, 'Pensées', in L Tolstoy (ed.), *A Calendar of Wisdom*, Alma Classics, U.K., p. 290.

49 Klein, M 1997, *Envy and Gratitude and other Works 1946–1963*, Vintage, London, p. 63.

50 ibid., p. 84.

51 Butler, D.S & Moseley, L 2003, *Explain Pain*, Noigroup Publications, Adelaide, Australia.

52 Klein, M 1997, *Envy and Gratitude and other Works 1946–1963*, p. 264.

53 ibid., p. 269.

54 Hinshelwood, R.D 1994, *Clinical Klein*, Free Association Books, London, p. 91.

55 Freud, S 1995, 'Mourning and melancholia', in P Gay (ed.), *The Freud reader*, Vintage Books, London, p. 584.

56 ibid., pp. 587-588.

57 Oster, E 2004, 'Witchcraft, Weather and Economic Growth in Renaissance Europe', *Journal of Economic Perspectives*, 18 (1), p. 216.

58 Seneca, LA 2011, *Letters from a Stoic*, Seedbox Press, Kindle Edition, location 631.

59 ibid., location 3151.

60 Campbell, J 1993, *The Hero with a Thousand Faces*, Fontana Press, London, p.36.

61 ibid, p.53.

62 ibid, pp. 52-53.

63 Jung, C.G. 1989, *Memories, Dreams, Reflections*, Vintage Books, U.S.A., p. 170.

64 Fine, C 2010, *Delusions of gender: the real science behind sex differences*, Icon Books Ltd., London, p. 177.

65 Waisberg, JL & Page, S 1988, 'Gender Role Nonconformity and Perception of Mental Illness', *Women & Health*, 14(1), pp. 3–16.

66 Horney, K 1999, *Neurosis and Human Growth: The Struggle Toward Self-Realisation*, Routledge, London, p. 242.

BEYOND THE PERSONAL

67 Frey-Rohn, L 1990, *From Freud to Jung: A Comparative Study of the Psychology of the Unconscious*, Shambala, Boston, MA p. 112.

68 Jung, C.G. 1990, *The Archetypes and the Collective Unconscious*, Princeton University Press, U.S.A, p. 63.

69 Smart, N 1979, *The Religious Experience of Mankind*, Fount Paperbacks, UK, p. 60.

70 Pascal, B 2008, *Human Happiness*, Penguin Books, London, p. 39.

71 Jung, C.G. 1990, *The Archetypes and the Collective Unconscious*, p. 62.

72 Murray, J. A. C. 1938, *An Introduction to Christian Psychotherapy*, T&T Clark, Edinburgh, p. 11.

73 Tolstoy, L 2005, *A Confession*, Dover Books, U.S.A., p. 17.

74 ibid., p. 21.

75 Jung, C.G. 1989, *Memories, Dreams, Reflections*, Vintage Books, U.S.A., p. 325.

76 Jung, C.G. 1975, 'Psychology and Religion: West and East', in H Read & G Adler (eds.), *The Collected Works of Carl Jung Volume 11*, Princeton University Press, New Jersey, p. 334.

77 For the sake of clarity, I've used the capitalised 'Self' to refer to our timeless, spiritual aspect that is distinct from our personality, ego, and anything of the world, though Jung's use of 'Self' included the wholeness of the personality.

78 Jung, C.G. 1989, *Memories, Dreams, Reflections*, p. 88.

79 ibid.

80 Campbell, J 1993, *The Hero with a Thousand Faces*, Fontana Press, London, pp. 131–133.

A COURSE IN MIRACLES

81 T-8.III.5:1-3

82 Though the Course's view of God ('First Cause') and His emanations, or 'creations', is genderless, the terms 'Him', 'Father', and 'Son' are used to define that which really can't be defined, and for the sake of clarity and consistency I also use the masculine pronouns to refer to God in the following discussion. For a detailed discussion of the Course's use of traditional Christian terminology along with masculine pronouns, I refer the interested reader to Kenneth Wapnick's book *A Talk Given on* A Course in Miracles*: An introduction*, (7th ed) pp. 41-44.

83 Smith, A.P 2008, *The Gnostics: History, Tradition, Scriptures, Influence*, Watkins Publishing, London, p. 93.

84 Wapnick, K 1990, *Love does not Condemn: The World, the Flesh, and the Devil According to Platonism, Christianity, Gnosticism, and A Course in Miracles*, Foundation for A Course in Miracles, New York, p. 388.

85 http://www.abc.net.au/news/2017-11-04/cross-to-bear-catholic-church-domestic-abuse/8680158

86 Freud, S 2013, *Civilization and its Discontents*, Kindle Edition, locations 676–677.

87 T-4.II.4:10-11.

88 Diogenes Laertius (1917), *The Lives and Opinions of Eminent Philosophers*, trans. WC Lawton, International Society, New York.

89 Aurelius, M, *The Meditations of Marcus Aurelius*, trans. G Long, Kindle Edition, location 131.

90 Gelman, M et al 2000, 'Viktor Emil Frankl 1905–1997', *American Journal of Psychiatry*, 157(4), p. 625.

91 Mother Teresa 1995, *A Simple Path*, Rider, London, p. 68.

92 ibid., p. 66.

93 Jung, C. G. 1990, *The Archetypes and the Collective Unconscious*, Princeton University Press, U.S.A., p. 21.

94 Jung, C.G. 2008, *C.G. Jung on Nature, Technology and Modern Life*, M Sabini (ed.), North Atlantic Books, U.S.A., pp. 215-216.

95 Ten-Boom, C 2009, *The Hiding Place*, Baker Publishing Group, Kindle Edition, locations 4746-4750.

96 Joyce, J 1982, *A Portrait of the Artist as a Young Man*, Granada, London, p. 186.

97 Emerson, RW 1969, *The Journals and Miscellaneous Notebooks of Ralph Waldo Emerson*, Vol. 7:1838-1842, AW Plumstead & H Hayford (eds.), The Belknap Press of Harvard University Press, U.S.A., p. 137.

98 Phaedo 100:d

99 Meyer, JE & Meyer R 1987, 'Self-Portrayal by a Depressed Poet: A Contribution to the Clinical Biography of William Cowper', *The American Journal of Psychiatry*, 144 (2), p. 128.

100 Sacks, O 2007, *Musicophilia: Tales of Music and the Brain*, Picador, UK, p. 299.

THE HOW OF FORGIVENESS

101 Lundin, RW 2015, *Alfred Adler's Basic Concepts and Implications*, Routledge, U.S.A., p. 62.

102 Adler, A 1998, *Understanding Human Nature*, Hazelden Foundation, U.S.A., p. 40.

103 Meister Eckhart 1994, *Selected Writings*, Penguin Classics, U.K., p. 7.

104 ibid., p. 27.

105 Mother Teresa 1995, *A Simple Path*, Rider, London, p. 91.

106 Green, H 1978, *I Never Promised you a Rose Garden*, Pan Books Ltd., London, pp. 155-165.

107 Blake, W 1970, 'The Everlasting Gospel', in J Bronowski (ed.), *William Blake: A Selection of Poems and Letters*, Penguin Books Australia, Ringwood, Victoria, p. 81.

108 Orwell, G 2004, *Why I Write*, Penguin Books Australia, Ringwood, Victoria, p. 4.

109 Salinger, JD 1991, *Franny and Zooey*, Little, Brown and Company, Boston, pp. 28–29.

110 Sacks, O 2015, 'My Own Life', *The New York Times*, p. 25.

111 Freud, S 1995, 'Wild Psychoanalysis', in P Gay (ed.), *The Freud Reader*, Vintage Books, London, p. 354.

THE DARK NIGHT OF THE SOUL

112 Underhill, E 1930, *Mysticism: A Study in the Nature and Development of Spiritual Consciousness*, Kindle Edition, locations 8948–8950.

113 Ramakrishna 2011, *The Original Gospel of Ramakrishna*, World Wisdom Books, Indiana, USA, p. 21.

114 Saint John of the Cross 2003, *The Dark Night of the Soul*, Dover Publications, Kindle Edition, p. 24.

115 Underhill, E 1914, *Practical Mysticism*, Waxkeep Publishing, Kindle Edition, p. 17.

116 Saint John of the Cross 2003, *The Dark Night of the Soul*, p. 51.

117 Underhill, E 1930, *Mysticism: A Study in the Nature and Development of Spiritual Consciousness*, locations 8680–8685.

118 Jung, C.G. 1990, *The Archetypes and the Collective Unconscious*, Princeton University Press, U.S.A., p. 121.

119 Guyon, J 1875, *Spiritual Torrents*, Trans. AW Marston, Marston, Low & Searle, London, Kindle Edition, p. 40.

120 Meister Eckhart 1994, *Selected Writings*, Penguin Classics, U.K., p. 22.

121 ibid., p. 23.

122 Dickson-Wright, C 2007, *Spilling the Beans*, Hodder & Stoughton, U.K., p. 182.

123 Jung, C.G. 1990, *The Archetypes and the Collective Unconscious*, p. 67.

124 Campbell, J 2011, *A Joseph Campbell Companion: Reflections on the Art of Living*, Joseph Campbell Foundation, Kindle Edition, p. 79.

125 Lewis, CS 2002, *Surprised by Joy*, Harper Collins Publishers, London, p. 16.

126 ibid., p. 7.

127 Nietzsche, F 2017, *Ecce Homo: How One Becomes What One is*, Translated by AM. Ludovici, LRP, Kindle Edition, locations 528-532.

128 Underhill, E 1930, *Mysticism: A Study in the Nature and Development of Spiritual Consciousness*, locations 3789-3790.

129 ibid., locations 3975-3978.

130 ibid., locations 8531-8534.

131 Emerson, RW 2012, *Self-Reliance and Other Essays*, Dover, U.S.A., p. 23.

132 Meister Eckhart 1994, *Selected Writings*, p. 9.

133 Underhill E 2013, *The spiritual life*, Martino Fine Books, Kindle Edition, locations 196-200.

134 Emerson, RW 1907, *Essays*, Merrill Co., New York, Kindle Edition, p. 131.

135 ibid.

136 Underhill, E 1930, *Mysticism: A Study in the Nature and Development of Spiritual Consciousness*, locations 9103–9108.

THE LIFE OF JANET FRAME

137 Frame, J 2008, *An Angel at my Table*, Random House Australia, Kindle Edition, location 614.

138 ibid., location 614.

139 King, M 2000, *Wrestling with the Angel: A Life of Janet Frame*, Picador, Sydney, p. 29.

140 Frame, J 2008, *An Angel at my Table*, location 893.

141 ibid., location 3414.

142 ibid., location 3709.

143 King, M 2000, *Wrestling with the Angel: A Life of Janet Frame*, p. 66.

144 ibid., p. 67.

145 Frame J, *An Angel at my Table*, locations 3773–3777.

146 ibid., location 3800.

147 ibid., locations 3799–3803.

148 ibid., locations 4404–4405.

149 ibid., location 3975.

150 ibid., location 4261.

151 ibid., location 4297.

152 ibid., location 4405.

153 ibid., locations 5036-5039.

154 King, M 2000, *Wrestling with the Angel: A Life of Janet Frame,* p. 90.

155 ibid., pp. 105–106.

156 Jung, C.G. 1990, *The Archetypes and the Collective Unconscious,* Princeton University Press, U.S.A., p. 21.

157 Guyon, J 1875, *Spiritual Torrents,* trans. AW Marston, Marston, Low & Searle, London, Kindle Edition, pp. 49–52.

158 Frame J, *An Angel at my Table,* location 1869.

159 ibid., location 2123.

160 ibid., locations 349–354.

161 Frame, J 2008, *Living in the Maniototo,* Vintage Books, Australia, p. 36.

162 Frame, J 2008, *An Angel at my Table,* locations 4419–4426.

163 ibid., location 4471.

164 ibid., location 7415.

165 ibid., location 8053.

166 ibid., location 217.

About the Author

Stephanie Panayi has worked as a Rolfer™ and counsellor, graduating from the Rolf Institute®, USA and Brazil, in 1998, and from Swinburne University, Australia, with a degree in psychology and psychophysiology, in 2004. A student of *A Course in Miracles* for twenty years, Stephanie integrated its principles within her professional practice and enjoys writing from a Course perspective.

Printed in Great Britain
by Amazon

13502899R00144